VEGETABLE GARDENING
for Beginners

T0151123

VEGETABLE GARDENING
for Beginners

Learn to Grow Anything No Matter Where You Live

SAMANTHA JOHNSON
AND
DANIEL JOHNSON

NEW SHOE PRESS

Inspiring | Educating | Creating | Entertaining

Brimming with creative inspiration, how-to projects, and useful information to enrich your everyday life, quarto.com is a favorite destination for those pursuing their interests and passions.

© 2023 Quarto Publishing Group USA Inc.
Text © 2012 Samantha Johnson and Daniel Johnson
Photography © 2012 Daniel Johnson

First Published in 2023 by New Shoe Press, an imprint of The Quarto Group, 100 Cummings Center, Suite 265-D, Beverly, MA 01915, USA.
T (978) 282-9590 F (978) 283-2742 Quarto.com

New Shoe Press titles are also available at discount for retail, wholesale, promotional, and bulk purchase. For details, contact the Special Sales Manager by email at specialsales@quarto.com or by mail at The Quarto Group, Attn: Special Sales Manager, 100 Cummings Center, Suite 265-D, Beverly, MA 01915, USA.

ISBN: 978-0-7603-8352-0
eISBN: 978-0-7603-8353-7

The content in this book was previously published in *The Beginner's Guide to Vegetable Gardening* (Voyageur Press 2012) by Samantha Johnson and Daniel Johnson.

Library of Congress Cataloging-in-Publication Data available

Photography: Daniel Johnson's collection, unless noted otherwise.

Acknowledgments

We would like to thank the following individuals who were particularly helpful during the process of writing this book. We could not have done it by ourselves!

- Our editors, Danielle Ibister and Elizabeth Noll, for all of their help and support! Thanks also to everyone at Voyageur Press for the opportunity to work on this project—thank you!

- Lorin for proofreading and advice on plastic garden covers; Paulette for photo editing, proofreading, and prep; Em and Anna for reading the manuscript and offering suggestions; and J. Keeler for proofing and noticing "a sentence that really didn't make any sense." Thanks!

- J. R.—for encouraging us in "green" pursuits.

- Cadi—because she likes to be mentioned.

- Myf—for being in charge of security.

- Gracie—for her joyous enthusiasm.

- Peaches—for just being cute.

- And to everyone who allowed Dan to photograph their garden—thank you!

To Mom,
our favorite gardener

Contents

Introduction

Welcome to Vegetable Gardening

It probably sounds funny, but it all started with one green pepper.

When we were kids, we lived in a little house on a lake, deep in the woods. There was not much sun and there were lots of deer, so we didn't have much of a vegetable garden. But one summer we had a little pepper plant in a pot, and after several weeks, the plant produced a single green bell pepper. The pepper was very small, but that didn't bother us. We were impressed by this green pepper that had appeared—almost magically!—on our plant, and we felt sure it rivaled any supermarket pepper.

Planting seeds, tending and nurturing seedlings, and growing food is an experience unlike any other. After our first taste of vegetable gardening, we just kept coming back for more, and we still enjoy the thrill of harvesting fresh vegetables. Dan enjoys growing potatoes (actually, Dan enjoys eating potatoes, but you have to grow them first!) and giant pumpkins. Samantha loves to experiment with different varieties of heirloom beans (this year she planted Empress, Speckled Cranberry, Hidatsa Shield Figure, and Dragon's Tongue) and she also likes growing cucumbers (crispy white ones—not those rubbery green things from the supermarket).

We also plant tomatoes, peas, onions, lettuce, squash, and carrots. Sometimes we grow cauliflower and broccoli, but we haven't been as successful with those, and we usually like to devote garden space to plants that are productive. We also make it a point not to grow vegetables that we don't like to eat, which is why Samantha refuses to grow lima beans (ugh!) even though she loves all other kinds of beans. Why waste garden space on something you can't stand to eat?

Our horses, ponies, and rabbits help our gardening pursuits by being super sources of compost, which keeps our garden soil full of nutrients.

Caring for your own garden and growing your own food will give you a level of enjoyment and satisfaction that's hard to find anywhere else—but it's also a lot of work. That's why we wrote this book: to guide you through the process of creating a vegetable garden. In these pages you'll find information on soil preparation, seed selection, planting, daily maintenance, and harvesting, as well as on cooking, selling, and exhibiting your produce.

It doesn't matter if your garden is big or small (remember, we started with one pepper plant!)—the important thing is to get started. Introduce yourself to the joys of vegetable gardening and experience the unique delight that comes from picking a ripe, red tomato and eating it while it's still warm from the sun.

Happy gardening!

Good soil, plenty of water, proper tools, and a lot of patience are the basics of good gardening. *Shutterstock*

Chapter 1

Planning Your Garden

Let's take a minute to talk about an important topic: Just where are you going to place your new garden?

Selecting a Garden Space

Before you rush out the front door and yell, "It's going here!" let's take a look at some factors that you might consider when picking out the perfect garden space.

Sunlight

All plants need some sunlight, and vegetable plants in particular require a lot. Figure on six to eight hours per day at minimum.

The ideal location for your vegetable garden will get plenty of sunshine.

Chances are you have never really watched your yard to see how the light hits it throughout the day. So do this: Pick a spot that you think would be a good candidate for your potential garden, and take note of how the sun shines on the area all during the day. (Cloudy days won't work because you can't really see where the area is shaded.) See if the location is in the sun at 9 o'clock in the morning, then at noon, and again at 5 o'clock in the evening. Did the spot stay sunny for the entire day, or did it become shaded at some point? Houses, sheds, garages, fences, and trees—even a tree quite far away—can cast shadows on your garden at certain times of the day, and you might not have ever noticed. If you find the area is heavily shaded for too much of the day, you'll have to find a new spot.

Water Access

Gardens—especially vegetable gardens—require a lot of water and most of this water must come from you. (Don't assume the rain will be enough.) Reasonably close access to an outdoor spigot is important. Of course, you can always buy multiple hoses and string them together, but this can get unwieldy (picture trying to coil up three or four hoses) and can also lead to poor water volume (the more hoses, the less water pressure you tend to get). If your perfect garden location is simply too far away to reach with a hose, you could always haul water in containers, but this is time-consuming and physically demanding. Water is heavy. It's better to plan on keeping the garden near a good water source. You can also try keeping a rain barrel to collect water from rooftops; this can be a great way of gathering water for your garden.

Drainage

On the other hand, too *much* water can cause major problems. Avoid planting your vegetable garden in low-lying areas where water collects for long periods. Ideally, you're looking for a nice flat piece of ground that will not become a puddle when it rains.

An outdoor spigot or water pump located within easy reach of your garden plot is not only convenient, but necessary.

Water access is an important consideration when selecting a garden location. In order to keep your garden well hydrated, you'll want a nearby water source.

Soaker hoses are the best way to water a vegetable garden. They're convenient and effective, and because they don't get the leaves wet, they help prevent disease.

Protection from Wind

Earlier we talked about the importance of sunlight and keeping your garden out in the open, away from objects that might cause shade. However, the complete absence of these objects can cause a different problem: wind. Big objects like trees and buildings can protect an area from wind, whereas in wide-open spaces, the wind can be quite hard on young plants, since they don't have a deep root system or strong stalks. This happens sometimes to our garden if a strong wind blows east or west. We have wind blocks to the north and south (they are far enough away not to shade the garden), but the east and west are open, and sometimes a gusty wind will come through early in the spring and bounce our poor little seedlings around pretty badly. So avoid open windy areas if you have a choice.

Safe to Dig?

You can't plant your garden in an area where there might be electric, utility, or water lines buried underground. Never dig unless you are absolutely sure that it's a safe area. Most states have a "Call Before You Dig" hotline that can tell you if utility lines are buried in your area.

This large garden has been designed with pathways and plenty of space to work comfortably.

This garden has been well organized so as to maximize the available space.

Size

Okay, so you've found the perfect garden space. Now you're faced with another decision: How big should it be?

The answer depends on your situation. How much work and how much time do you want to put into a garden? It can be rather defeating to start out with high expectations (a garden that's too large) only to find that your plans were too ambitious. Plant a garden slightly smaller than you think you will need. This will help keep your goals realistic. For starters, you might try an 8 × 10-foot garden, or a pair of 4 × 10-foot raised beds. If you're feeling a bit more ambitious, expand to a 10 × 16-foot garden, and if you want to really give yourself plenty of space, opt for a 20 × 40-foot garden. Our garden is approximately 900 square feet (30 × 30 feet), and in the spring, when we're planting and preparing, we spend a lot of time in it—a few hours each day. Later on, during the summer months, it doesn't require as much time. A smaller garden (6 × 10) would require less time per day, and the time spent weeding would literally be just minutes per week.

Fencing that is primarily decorative, as in the two photos on this page, still serves a purpose—it separates one garden area from another, or from the rest of the yard. *iStockphoto.com/April M. Taulbee*

Fencing can be as simple or as elaborate as you choose. This deer-proof fence is extremely practical but also attractive.

Fencing

You may decide to fence in your garden. Few things look better than a well-groomed garden with lovely paths and a pretty fence going all the way around. But there are also practical reasons for a fence, such as keeping out large animals (deer) or small ones (rabbits and gophers).

If you're borrowing or using an existing garden plot (perhaps a family or community garden), your fence problems may already be taken care of. However, if you're starting from scratch, you're going to have to consider a few things, not the least of which is getting some help. Fencing of any sort is a big job, and doing it properly can take a lot of time, effort, and skill. Because there are so many different types of fencing, for so many purposes, we can't cover them all here. But these pointers will help you figure out what kind of a fence you need.

Fence Options

Decorative fence. Is the fence just for looks? Or perhaps you're trying to define the garden area as being separate from the rest of the lawn or landscaping. If this is the case, just about any fence you can think of (or can build easily) might suffice.

Rabbit-proof fence. Will your area be bothered by rabbits? These critters can wreak havoc in your garden. Keep out rabbits with a fence that has 1-inch wire mesh and is at least a couple of feet high. Push the fence an inch or two into the soil to prevent little ones from slipping underneath.

Ground squirrel-proof fence. Keeping out very small burrowing animals like ground squirrels (also known as gophers) will require ½-inch mesh (they can squeeze through the tiniest openings). The bottom edge of the mesh will need to be buried 12 inches under the ground to keep the little guys from burrowing under the fence.

Deer-proof fence. Preventing damage from larger animals like deer requires a very tall fence—at least 6 feet tall. Building a fence of this magnitude is a huge task that will involve a lot of effort and expense and is not a job to go into alone.

Raised Beds

A raised bed is a garden plot that is higher than the ground around it. The height can vary from six inches to two feet or more. You fill up this bed with good garden soil—either store-bought or a mixture of your own creation using topsoil and organic material.

Why plant vegetables in a raised bed? There are a couple of reasons. For one, a raised bed dries out quicker than a garden in the ground for the simple reason that gravity is pulling the water down. If you live in a fairly wet region with frequent heavy rainfall, a raised bed can help drain away this excess water more quickly. Raised beds also warm up faster in the spring, so they can lengthen your growing season.

Another reason to use raised beds is if your soil is just too difficult to work with. Perhaps you have too much sand or clay. A raised bed can let you start over from scratch with soil that you know will grow fantastic vegetables.

A raised bed can be any size you like, but 4 × 8 feet is a common choice. This size allows you to easily reach to the middle of the bed without having to go in and step on the soil. This will help keep your ground soft and workable.

You can build a raised bed out of rocks, wood, cement block, or other materials. Wood is probably the most commonly used. You will need lumber for this, such as 2 × 6s or 2 × 8s placed on their edges and built into a square or rectangular frame. This might be the easiest part of building a raised bed; the hard part will be hauling the soil and filling in the frame.

These gardeners are preparing for spring planting. The raised bed in the foreground is not quite finished; more soil is necessary in order to raise the soil level.

This wire mesh is an example of a simple fence that is very easy to install, yet still serves its purpose, which is to keep out rabbits.

A garden cloche is a wonderful way to protect your plants from cold weather while making your garden a prettier place. This adorable West Highland white terrier also makes a nice addition to the garden scene.

Cold Frames and Cloches

Cold frames and cloches are like miniature greenhouses; you can use them to protect plants from either an early or a late frost. There are all kinds of styles you can buy or build, but they all work by using some kind of transparent material (glass, fiberglass, or durable plastic) to let sunlight in, hold the warmth, and keep the cold out. A cloche is a smaller (often glass) "lid" that you can put over a smaller plant at night, while a cold frame is a larger bottomless box that can protect larger (and more) plants. Be aware that cold frames and cloches may need to be opened during the day if the temperatures are warm; otherwise it will become too hot or humid inside.

NOTE:

Cold frames and cloches are like miniature greenhouses; you can use them to protect plants from either an early or a late frost.

Gardening in Small Spaces

Even if you live in an urban or suburban area, you can have a garden. In fact, it may be a lot easier than you think to get started nurturing your green thumb. Growing vegetables in containers is a simple and effective way to grow some of your own food without needing to establish a garden plot in your yard. (See page 22.)

If you do have a small yard, then the world of outdoor gardening awaits! You may be amazed by the quantity of vegetables that a 10 × 10-foot garden can produce; in fact, if you employ special techniques, such as succession planting, you could easily double or triple your garden yield in the same 10 × 10-foot space. (See page 54.)

Another option that is rapidly gaining momentum is the community garden. This remarkable idea is beginning to take off, and community gardens are sprouting up (pun intended) all across the country. The idea behind a community garden is to provide a place for local gardeners to come together and grow vegetables. The use of a plot of land is typically donated, and fencing, garden beds, garden tools, and a water source are provided, often courtesy of sponsorships from local businesses or families. Interested gardeners typically pay a small fee to work a small portion of the community garden where they plant their own personal vegetables. An added benefit of a community garden is the camaraderie. Community gardens provide an opportunity for local families to participate in the growth of their own food, which might not have been a feasible option otherwise.

Tools of the Trade

A gardener's tools are extremely important, and you'll have an easier time gardening if you have at least a few of the proper tools to work with.

Rake. The gardener's best friend, your rake will be with you through thick and thin. A metal rake with short teeth is just what you need.

Garden gloves. We list these first because they are such a fundamental item for gardening. You'll want a good pair of gardening gloves sturdy enough to hold up through a lot of hard work, yet thin enough that you can comfortably function without it seeming as though you can't feel anything.

Hoe. Another important tool, ranked just slightly below the rake in importance.

Shovel. Also handy to have around is a larger, full-size shovel for digging larger quantities of dirt, such as when planting rhubarb or asparagus.

Soaker hose. Soaker hoses are the best choice for watering your garden.

Scissors. Ordinary desk scissors will do nicely; you'll want to keep a pair handy.

Watering can. Self-explanatory, we think.

Hose with a spray-head. Handy for aiming the water exactly where you want it to go (not on the leaves).

Garden claw. Useful for turning your soil and giving it one final loosening before you plant—ever so helpful!

Trowel. A small, handheld shovel that is just perfect for digging holes, a trowel will be helpful in a variety of situations, including transplanting seedlings.

Wheelbarrow. Another tool that you will use constantly, whether you're hauling soil, removing rocks, or cleaning up at the end of the season.

Hand fork. A hand fork is a three-tined "rake" that fits comfortably in your hand. Keep it with your trowel, as you'll use them together.

Obviously, there are many, many other tools and gadgets that you can use to make your gardening life easier, but this basic set of tools will get you started. As you continue gardening, you'll develop a good idea of which tools you constantly rely on and which tools end up gathering cobwebs and dust in the shed.

The initial monetary investment in your tools can be as large or as small as your budget allows. A set of quality tools will last you for years, so buy the best tools you can afford.

Container Gardening

What if you just don't have the space for a true in-the-ground garden? Perhaps your home doesn't have any yard space, and you are unable to beg, borrow, or rent ground anywhere else that's convenient. Are you out of luck?

iStockphoto.com/bgwalker

Of course not—you still have pots! There are many types of vegetables that will grow just fine in containers. They take up minimal space, require less work than a full-size garden, and still produce tasty delights.

A potted vegetable can fit into just about any sunlit place: a porch, a balcony, a large sunny window. Now, granted, you probably won't be growing corn indoors, but you can achieve some small-scale success with other vegetables. Here are a few ideas to get you started:

- **Peas**. Try the Tom Thumb variety for top quality in a dwarf pea package. You can easily grow Tom Thumb peas in containers.
- **Tomatoes**. Choose a determinate variety, one that will mature to a limited size while still producing a high quantity of tomatoes. Did you know that tomatoes can also be grown upside down? You can make your own upside-down planter from a five-gallon bucket, or you can buy the Topsy Turvy® planter, which is designed to be hung upside down. This is a fun and unusual way of growing tomatoes in a container!
- **Herbs**. The perfect choice for container gardening, herbs are fragrant, useful, delicious, and grow beautifully in their little pots. Keep a taste of summer in your kitchen all winter long.
- **Peppers**. Why not? Give sweet or hot peppers a chance. You might be surprised at how well they handle container life.
- **Root crops**. Now, obviously you won't be able to fit very many in a small container, but you can certainly grow a few carrots or radishes in a pot.

The key to container gardening is to keep them where they can obtain sunshine, keep them well watered and well drained (drainage holes in the bottom of your containers are required), and make sure that your containers are of sufficient size. Aim for a pot at least 16 inches deep and 12 inches in diameter for most vegetables.

Another important consideration is the soil. Purchase "container mix" from a garden center. This type of product is formulated to include exactly what is necessary for proper plant growth, and it's free of the bacteria that are sometimes found in regular garden soil.

Planting in pots can also extend your growing season. You can start planting far earlier in the year because you won't have to wait for the ground to warm or the frosty nights to end. Likewise, in the fall, you can dodge the killing frosts by simply bringing the pots inside on the cold nights and putting them back out in the morning. Your vegetables will continue to flourish long after everyone else has given up for the season.

Planning Ahead: Next Year's Garden

When fall is over and your garden has been harvested and your tools put away for the year, it's a good time to think about what changes you'd like to make for next year.

Size

How did the size of your garden work out this year? Was it big enough to include everything you wanted to grow? Or was it too big and ended up being more work than you wanted to do? Make note of your answers and take that into consideration when planning for next year.

What to Plant

You probably had some vegetables that you enjoyed a lot, other vegetables not so much. Or you might've found some types of vegetables that grew well in your location and others that didn't. All this should be taken into account when planning for next year. Eliminate the disappointments and use that space for new varieties of something that did work well. Or try something totally new.

Crop Rotation

Crop rotation is an important concept to understand. Plants use up particular resources within the soil each year, while at the same time, they also replenish other resources. If you insist on planting the same type of plant in the same spot year after year, pretty soon that spot will be drained of some resources and overabundant with others. This can lead to poor crop production.

The other reason you should rotate crops is to control diseases and insects. If a particular plant, say peppers, becomes infected with a disease during the year, that disease may stay in the soil all winter and infect next year's peppers. Moving the vegetables around helps keep your new pepper plants free of disease. For instance, after planting carrots, plant peas; the year after a corn crop, plant tomatoes in the same place. It's very helpful to learn the basics of vegetable "families" so that you don't inadvertently make a crop rotation mistake. You might think that planting eggplant after tomatoes would be a safe option, but eggplant and tomatoes are both from the nightshade family, so this would not be a wise rotation selection.

> **TIP**
>
> Crop rotation is an important concept to understand. Certain vegetables can deplete the soil of certain nutrients, and since the vast majority of vegetables are annuals and have to be replanted each year anyway, it's wise to move them around to new locations.

Peppers are from the nightshade family, along with potatoes, tomatoes, and eggplant. When you rotate your crops, be sure the new plants are from a different family than last year's crop.

At the end of the season, ask yourself: Was my garden too large? Too small? Just right? Then make adjustments for next year.

Photosynthesis

Everybody knows that plants need three things to grow: soil, water, and sunlight. But how on earth do the plants do it? How can dirt, water, and light become leaves, roots, and vegetables? The process has the tongue-twisting name of *photosynthesis*.

Photosynthesis is a complicated process, but, basically, it works like this:

1. Every green portion of a plant contains light-collecting pigments called chlorophyll. The plant's leaves collect the most light (because of their shape and size). When the sun shines onto the chlorophyll, the plant seizes energy from the sun.
2. Water is taken in by the plant's roots, and carbon dioxide (a gas that is in the air all around us) is absorbed from the air.
3. Using the energy from the sunlight, the plant combines the water and carbon dioxide to create carbohydrates—essentially, food for all parts of the plant.
4. During the photosynthesis process, there is some leftover material from the water and carbon dioxide. This material is expelled into the air as oxygen.

Parts of a Plant

Let's take a closer look at plants in general and vegetable plants in particular. All plants share a basic structure, and it's a good idea to become familiar with these parts and how they help the plant grow.

- **Roots**. The root system dives into the ground and becomes a base for which the plant can hold on. In addition to giving the plant a strong hold with the earth, the root system searches for water and minerals, both of which are pulled up into the plant for further use.

- **Stem**. The stem is the backbone of a plant. It connects the roots with the leaves, fruit, and blossoms.

- **Leaves**. The leaves of a plant are sunlight collectors. Like the stem, the leaves contain a green pigment called chlorophyll that is used for harvesting the sun's energy. Leaves collect more energy than the stem simply because they have more surface area.

- **Blossoms**. The flowers of a plant.

- **Fruit**. The actual end product of the plant's work, formed after the blossom. This is the part we eat. Squash, pumpkins, tomatoes, beans, and peas are all examples of vegetable "fruit." However, depending on the vegetable, we may eat *all parts of the plant*, not just the fruit. (In many cases, the actual fruit is not used at all.) What parts are eaten? Take a look:

  - **Roots**. Many vegetables are actually the plant's roots. Carrots, radishes, and parsnips are all root crops.

  - **Stems**. Pass me the celery.

  - **Leaves**. Lettuce and spinach are really just leaves.

  - **Flowers**. Cauliflower and broccoli are flower buds.

Blossoms

Leaves

Fruit

Stem

Roots

Vegetable Families

FAMILY NAME	VEGETABLES
Alliaceae	Onions, Garlic, Chives
Apiaceae	Parsley, Carrots, Dill, Parsnips
Amaranthaceae	Beets, Spinach
Brassicaceae	Broccoli, Brussels Sprouts, Cabbage, Cauliflower, Radishes
Cucurbitaceae	Cucumbers, Squash, Pumpkins
Fabaceae	Peas, Beans
Poaceae	Corn
Solanaceae	Potatoes, Tomatoes, Eggplant, Peppers

Heirloom tomatoes aren't very resistant to disease, so be sure to rotate your crops every spring.

Extending Your Growing Season the Easy Way

One way to extend your season in spring and fall is to make use of plastic covers. The plastic works well to keep the ground warm underneath the plastic, while also protecting tender plants from dangerous frosts.

Purchase ultraviolet-resistant plastic from garden centers or online. Or you can use clear plastic, which can be purchased from your local home center and will easily last a growing season.

Keep your frame simple. Use wood that's 1 × 4 inches or 2 × 2 inches and fasten the pieces together with woodscrews.

Place the plastic cover over the frames, draping it onto the ground and holding it down with rocks or boards. Space your frames about 4 feet apart. This system is simple and allows easy access to the garden. Remove the plastic after the temperatures have warmed sufficiently and there is no danger of frost.

Community gardens are a great way to start gardening if you live in an urban or suburban area.

Chapter 2

Getting Started

As a gardener, you have many ways to increase your chances for success in your garden. You can choose a suitable garden location, build good soil, provide regular water, and know what to plant and when. Many other aspects can play a part in whether or not your garden is successful, but one thing you can't change is your climate. Because the climate of your area plays such an important part in your gardening experience, we're going to start off by discussing growing seasons. We'll also discuss sources for you to obtain local help for your gardening project.

Growing Seasons

Generally speaking, the growing season is the length of time between frosts: the time between the last frost of spring until the first frost of fall. The length of time between the two dates varies extensively by location. At the tip of Florida, the growing season is nearly year-round; in northern Minnesota, it is usually only a few months, or approximately 120 days. You need to select plants that are able to mature within your growing season or take measures to extend your growing season artificially.

Knowledge of your growing season is necessary to avoid planting too early in the spring. If your area's average date of last spring frost is June 1, you wouldn't want to plant your tender seedlings on May 1, only to have them damaged by a hard frost a few weeks later. On the other hand, knowing your average last date of frost will help you pinpoint when to begin sowing your first seeds. Carrots, beets, peas, and other cold-hardy crops can be sown as soon as the ground can be worked in the spring.

Peas are one of the easiest vegetables to grow. They do best when planted in early spring, while the temperatures are still cool, which makes them suitable for growing even in regions with short growing seasons.

Here is a community garden in Zone 3 during the summer months. Despite the short growing season that exists in this zone, this garden is doing well. Starting seeds early indoors and using row covers are good ways to extend the growing season.

TIP

You need to select plants that are able to mature within your growing season or take measures to extend your growing season artificially.

There are ways to extend your growing season. Starting your seeds indoors in the early spring can give you an excellent jumpstart on the growing season as opposed to sowing directly into the ground in the late spring. Greenhouses, hoop houses, cold frames, cloches, and row covers are additional ways to add a few weeks onto each end of your growing season.

The most important thing to remember is to work *with* your climate rather than fighting against it. If you live in a cloudy climate, put your garden in the location that receives the most sunlight for the longest amount of time per day. If you live in a dry climate, be sure that you have a water source nearby to make it easy to water your garden each day.

If you live in a dry climate, you must have a good watering system in place. In this garden, soaker hoses have been set up to provide regular watering.

Your Climate

Your area's climate plays a part in your gardening too. Perhaps you live in a very dry region that receives little rain. In this case, you will have more success raising crops that are well suited to drier climates—peppers and tomatoes, for instance. On the other hand, if you live in a region that receives a great deal of precipitation, you might have success with vegetables that thrive in wetter soil—lettuce, for instance, or carrots. (The growing specifications of each vegetable are discussed more thoroughly in Chapter 5.)

The amount of sunshine is also important. All vegetables require an ample amount of sunshine, so a person living in a climate with plenty of sun may have an easier time growing vegetables than someone in a cloudy climate.

Sunshine is very important for the success of a vegetable garden. Keep this in mind when selecting a garden location.

Seasons

We all know that the Earth spins on its axis, creating night and day as alternate sides face the sun, and that it also makes a full circle around the sun once a year. But what about seasons? What causes them?

The answer lies in the Earth's axis tilt. Imagine a stick pointing straight through the Earth, starting at the South Pole and coming out at the North Pole. This is the Earth's axis. As the Earth spins (once a day), this "stick" remains stationary. You would think this stick would be straight up and down, but it isn't; it's tilted to one side just a bit at an angle of 23.5 degrees. All by itself, this tilt doesn't do much to our climate on a daily basis, but once you add in the Earth's annual travels around the sun, things start to get interesting. The tilt allows certain parts of the Earth to take full advantage of the sun's power at certain times of the year, but also ensures that other parts of the Earth receive *less* power. It works like this:

Let's say it's a hot July day in the United States, perhaps North Dakota. The United States is in the northern hemisphere of the Earth, and during July, the Earth's axis tilt is positioned in such a way that the northern hemisphere is pointing directly at the sun. The tilt also causes the length of the day to be quite long and the night relatively short—meaning we receive more heat. It's summer in North Dakota. But now let's imagine the very same day in Bolivia, a country in South America. Bolivia is in the southern hemisphere of the Earth, and the southern hemisphere isn't pointed at the sun in July. The days are shorter, the nights longer, and the temperatures generally colder. It's winter in Bolivia. The situation changes as the Earth travels around the sun and the months pass. Slowly, the tilt causes the southern hemisphere of the Earth to swing back toward the sun, while the northern hemisphere drifts back into the shadows. Eventually, by late December, the situation has reversed itself completely, with North Dakota buried under heavy snowfalls and chilled by frigid temperatures, and Bolivia enjoying hot sunshine. However, seasonal variations in the southern hemisphere are generally milder than those in the northern.

If there were no axis tilt, we wouldn't have seasonal changes, and many locations that enjoy excellent growing conditions during the summer would be too cold for gardening all of the time.

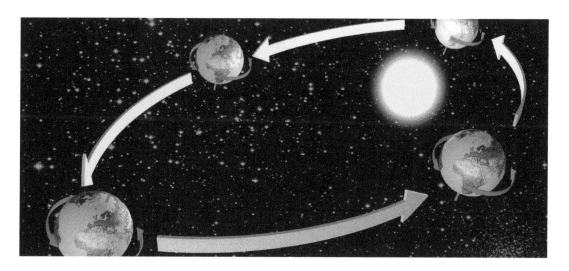

Learning the Ropes

You can't expect to be a gardening expert instinctively. This book provides you with a lot of information and advice, but we always recommend that you enlist the help of a local mentor to assist you with your vegetable gardening project. Someone with knowledge of your particular climate and zone will be able to give you detailed insight and guidance that we simply cannot provide.

Excellent sources to try include:

Other gardeners. Does your aunt Martha keep a vegetable garden? How about your next-door neighbor? Friends and family who have gardening experience can be helpful to you as you get started with your gardening project. You can take advantage of their years of practice (and learn from their failed experiments!) by asking a lot of questions and following their advice.

It's wise to obtain assistance from other local gardeners; a relative, perhaps, or a neighbor. Their knowledge of growing conditions in your region will be a benefit to you as you begin your gardening project.

Community gardens. If there is a local community garden in your area, then you may want to consider participating, especially if you're just starting out with your vegetable gardening project. A community garden is a large plot of garden space that is shared by the members of a community. Aside from the benefits of camaraderie and fellowship, you'll also benefit from the opportunity to share equipment and experience.

Local cooperative extension agents. These knowledgeable individuals can be very helpful to you in learning more about your climate and zone. In addition, extension agents can assist you in performing soil tests to identify potential mineral deficiencies, and they can provide you with advice and literature to study. To find your nearest cooperative extension office, visit www.usda.gov or call 202-720-4423.

Local nurseries. Visiting garden centers or nurseries in your area can be a good way to get advice on which vegetables (and other plants) are well suited to your location and zone. If you're stopping there to shop anyway, be sure to ask questions. The selection is often more limited than mail-order, but it can be more convenient. Also, it's nice to browse—to look at the plants or seeds in person rather than on a screen.

Master gardeners. Don't overlook the obvious! Your own county's master gardener program can be a good resource for gardening advice.

Community gardens can be a wonderful way to begin gardening, especially if you don't have the space to put in a garden at home.

The condition of your garden soil is very important to the success (or failure!) of your garden. Contact your local extension service for a soil test kit.

Local nurseries are a great place to talk with knowledgeable individuals who are familiar with the nuances of gardening in your particular area. *iStockphoto.com/Terry Healy*

Don't be too shy to ask for help. Here's a secret: gardeners love to give advice. They are thrilled to tell you about the lessons they learned the hard way. Find a handful of people to guide you through the first few seasons—and beyond.

No matter how many people help you, the success of your garden is ultimately in your hands. Some say that the best mulch is a gardener's time—meaning that the more time you spend caring for your garden, the more satisfying your results will be. *iStockphoto.com/Chris Price*

Chapter 3

Digging In

Selecting your seeds and seedlings is one of the best parts of gardening. In this chapter, we'll discuss starting from seed, purchasing seedlings, heirlooms and hybrids, perennials and annuals, and lots of other things that will put you well on your way to a great garden.

Where to Buy?

Seed Catalogs

In January, while the snow swirls madly outside and the temperature drops to a frigid level, something magical happens. The seed catalogs begin to arrive. You'll find them one day when you open up your mailbox: a colorful compendium of horticultural delight in the form of a sea of seed catalogs.

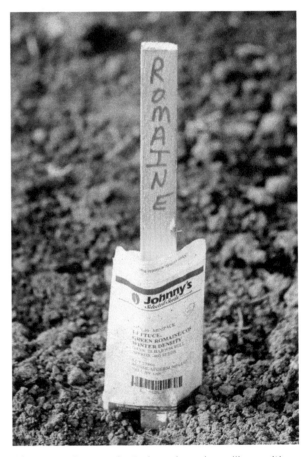

Always mark your planted seeds and seedlings with a small stake.

There is a great deal of satisfaction in watching seeds grow into healthy seedlings.

If you don't already receive seed catalogs, simply ask for them. If you search for "seed catalog" online, you'll be amazed by the number of companies that sell seeds and seedlings. Visit the websites of the companies that interest you and click the "request catalog" button. In no time, you'll have seed catalogs of your very own to brighten the wintry days. Many people prefer to leisurely browse through a print catalog as opposed to shopping online—and if you're seriously trying to determine your planting plans, a seed catalog to look through again and again will undoubtedly be helpful. (See Appendix 3: Resources, page 140.)

In addition to their colorful photographs and fascinating descriptions, seed catalogs serve an important use: They have ample varieties from which to choose. Your local nurseries may only be able to provide you with limited varieties, whereas seed catalogs offer everything under the sun, which gives you the opportunity to purchase and plant exactly what you want for your specific location and needs.

Pay attention when the catalogs arrive, as some seed companies send discount coupons with the catalogs. Note the expiration date so that you can use the coupons before they expire.

Online Nurseries

Not all seed companies produce a print catalog. Some offer their products online only, but don't let this deter you from browsing their available products. Although an actual catalog can be easier, don't overlook the companies that exist solely online; they may offer seed varieties that you can't obtain elsewhere.

Seed catalogs make wonderful winter reading. Imagine the possibilities for the upcoming garden season—not just vegetables, but maybe fruit trees, flowers, and more!

Local Nurseries and Garden Centers

For convenience, you can't top a local garden center or nursery. They are also perfect for spontaneous garden decisions, such as: "I want to plant spaghetti squash *today*, and I want seedlings rather than seeds." In as long as it takes to drive to the garden center and select your seedlings, you can have the satisfaction of bringing home and planting your spaghetti squash seedlings. You can't achieve this kind of immediate gratification from a seed catalog or an online nursery.

There are other benefits from purchasing your seeds or seedlings locally. You can pretty much count on the fact that the varieties offered for sale will be suitable for growing in your area. Additionally, garden center employees can provide you with helpful information about selecting the best plants to suit your needs.

If you're looking to get started in a hurry, just pop over to your local garden center or nursery. You might find what you're looking for—and you won't have to pay for shipping.

Plant Sales

You might see plants for sale in a lot of other places, too. Yard sales, farmers' markets, and roadside stands are all places where plants are sold. You'll have to rely on your best judgment when purchasing from unknown sources. Do the plants look healthy, strong, and free of disease?

TIP

Seed packets are an affordable way to experiment with many different vegetable varieties.

When you're shopping for vegetable plants at a garden center, don't worry if you get sidetracked in the flower department. Adding a few flowers to your vegetable garden encourages bees and other pollinators to visit. *Shutterstock*

Starting from Seeds

If your garden project is on a budget, then starting from seed is undoubtedly the most inexpensive way to get started. Seed packets are an affordable way to experiment with many different vegetable varieties. The average seed packet costs less than the price of a single seedling, and one seed packet could potentially provide you with dozens of plants. For instance, a package of Gold Medal tomato seeds from Seed Savers Exchange costs $2.75, and a Gold Medal tomato seedling costs $3. That $2.75 packet contains fifty seeds, which could potentially produce fifty plants, a value of $150.

Having said that, seeds do not give you the head start that seedlings do, which can be a problem if you are in a climate with a short growing season. This means that rather than sowing your seeds directly into the ground, you will want to consider starting the seeds indoors several weeks before your scheduled planting date.

You can usually purchase seeds in two quantities: packets or bulk. Seed packets are what you see on the shelves at your local hardware store or even in your grocery store: tiny envelopes with about twenty-five to fifty seeds inside. Bulk seeds can be purchased in quantities up to one ounce or even one pound.

Plant sales usually don't have the selection that you'll find at a garden center, but you might be surprised at what you find to take home.

There are advantages to both methods of purchase. Small seed packets are less expensive upfront, and they are a great way to experiment with a new variety on a small scale. You can test it out, see how it grows for you, see how it tastes, and then decide whether you would like to dedicate a larger portion of your garden to growing more of that variety in future years. Buying in bulk is more expensive upfront, but the actual cost per seed is less. For example, you can buy 500 of the same Gold Medal tomato seeds for $10.75 or an ounce (nearly 14,000 seeds) for $44. If you have a particular variety that you really like, and you have a very large garden or a small farm, then buying seed in bulk is the most economical way to plant.

Starting Seeds Indoors

Let's say that Bert has his heart set on planting Jumbo Pink Banana squash—an intriguing type of heirloom winter squash. The seed packet says that Jumbo Pink Banana squash will require 105 days to reach maturity. Unfortunately, Bert lives in a region where the average last date of frost is mid-June, and his first frost of the season is usually in mid-September. Count up the days and it's less than 100. Bert doesn't see how he can

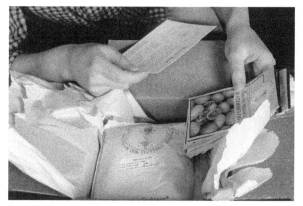

You can order seeds in packets or in bulk, as shown here. If you have a very large garden, and you want to plant a lot of one variety, you'll buy seed in bulk.

possibly grow Jumbo Pink Banana squash by starting the seeds directly outdoors. So Bert decides to get his seeds started indoors.

Starting seeds indoors is one of the best ways to extend your growing season by several weeks. It gives you a head start so that by the time the weather has warmed up enough to actually put your plants outdoors, your little seedlings may have already had eight to ten weeks of advance growing time.

Seed-starting kits are one of the easiest ways to get started with seeds indoors. The kits usually provide plastic trays (known as flats), the "plugs" of compacted growing compound (nice because they don't spill everywhere, as potting soil is apt to do), and plastic covers to increase warmth and expedite germination.

This is not to say that you can't make your own seed-starting containers using cups, cans, pots, or the like. You'll just want to make sure they are very clean and have small holes for drainage. You'll also need to provide plenty of light, either natural or artificial, to grow healthy seedlings.

Germination

Indoors or out, one of the most exciting parts of planting seeds is waiting for them to sprout. What's better than seeing the first round leaves unfolding in the miracle of new life?

But how long will you have to wait? It depends on a number of variables. Some vegetables simply germinate faster than others do. Radishes are quick to pop up: You might see them in five days. Others, like beets, might take two weeks to pop out of the ground. A good rule of thumb is to allow seven to ten days for germination. There are other factors, of course. Cold soil that has not warmed sufficiently will delay the germination of many vegetable seeds. Hard-packed soil can also delay germination, which is why tilling can be so important. Old seed can take longer to germinate than fresh seed; be sure to use fresh seed. And finally, if you plant your seeds deeper than the recommended depth, this could delay their germination.

In seven to ten days, these seeds will be sprouting and the fun will begin.

Speeding Up Your Seeds: The Basics of Soaking

If you want to boost the speed of germination, try soaking your seeds before you plant them. This is easy enough to accomplish; just take a shallow dish, place your seeds on it, and submerge the seeds in warm water. Leave the seeds in the water overnight and plant them the next day.

Peat Pots

Peat pots are an ingenious way to transplant sensitive plants from indoors to the ground without disturbing their tender roots. The small pots are biodegradable and can simply be planted directly into the ground without removing the pot. Make several vertical slices in the pot before planting, to help roots grow out more easily. Sensitive seedlings such as winter squash, watermelon, and cauliflower are all good candidates for starting in peat pots.

When you order seedlings via mail-order, be sure to open the box immediately. Your new seedlings will need air and water. Keep them in the shade until you're ready to plant.

These small sunflower seedlings have their cotyledon leaves and are just beginning to get their true leaves.

Starting from Seedlings

If you don't want to start from seed outdoors and would prefer not to start your seeds indoors, then you may decide to purchase seedlings. Local nurseries are the easiest place to obtain seedlings, but you can also purchase seedlings from catalogs or online nurseries. The seedlings are then shipped directly to you. When you purchase locally, you can hand-select the individual seedlings, choosing the best and strongest specimens. Additionally, you eliminate any chance of the seedlings being damaged in transit. However, most companies strive to ship only the best seedlings and package the seedlings carefully. We have had excellent success in purchasing seedlings through mail-order.

It can be tricky to select seedlings. It's common to go for the tallest ones at the garden center. Many people think that taller seedlings are obviously more mature than a shorter specimen. Actually, the taller seedlings are not considered to be the best choices for transplanting. Shorter seedlings with more substance to their stems are likely to be hardier and more suitable for transplanting.

You may need to "harden off" your new seedlings in order to acclimate them before planting—over a period of one to two weeks, increase the time they are outside, from a few hours to overnight.

Your seedlings will probably need to be acclimated (called "hardening off") before planting. The average temperature inside the greenhouse at your local garden center may be quite a bit warmer than the temperature of your garden at night. You can harden off your seedlings by placing them outdoors for a few hours during the day, then steadily increase their time outside and slowly introduce them to cooler temperatures before leaving them out overnight and then planting them. This process usually takes between one and two weeks, assuming that the weather is cooperating and all chance of frost is past.

Annuals Versus Perennials

A simple definition of a perennial is a plant that survives for more than two growing seasons; an annual is a plant that does not. This means that if you plant a perennial, you can look forward to enjoying its renewed life each and every spring. On the other hand, your annual plants will have to be replaced every year. Generally speaking, vegetables are annuals (a couple of exceptions are asparagus and rhubarb); many flowers and herbs are perennials. In Chapter 5, we'll describe which vegetables are annuals and which are perennials.

Heirlooms Versus Hybrids

A few years ago, the term *heirloom vegetable* was not a part of many people's vocabularies. People were more familiar with hybrid vegetables, which are the genetic crossing of two distinctly different plants, resulting in a plant with increased hardiness and disease resistance but lacking in the ability to reproduce itself identically from its seeds.

Hybrid vegetables are very popular with gardeners. Many varieties have been developed to meet specific needs, such as early-maturing tomatoes or disease-resistant cucumbers. Over time, the dominance of hybrids caused the traditional heirloom varieties to be virtually eclipsed. As years passed, the best hybrids became the favored choice of gardeners, while the unique heirloom varieties were nearly forgotten.

Thankfully, gardeners have rallied together to save heirloom varieties from extinction, and today heirlooms are thriving once again. Many people still think that all tomatoes are round and red, but heirloom enthusiasts are spreading the word that tomatoes can also be found in green, yellow, orange, pink, and purple and

TIP

Many people think that taller seedlings are obviously more mature than a shorter specimen. Actually, the taller seedlings are not considered to be the best choices for transplanting. Shorter seedlings with more substance to their stems are likely to be hardier and more suitable for transplanting.

in a wide variety of sizes and shapes. They may not have the hardiness or disease resistance of newer hybrids, but heirlooms are a vital part of our vegetable heritage. Generally speaking, heirloom vegetables are open pollinated, meaning that their seeds breed true, while the seeds of hybrids do not. Additionally, there is a delightful range of flavors, shapes, and colors to be found within heirloom varieties; for instance, you simply haven't tasted perfection until you've tried a perfectly ripe Wapsipinicon Peach tomato!

Peas, like most vegetables, are an annual rather than a perennial.

TIP

A few years ago, the term *heirloom vegetable* was not a part of many people's vocabulary, but now many gardeners are experimenting with the amazing variety of sizes, shapes, and colors they offer.

Hybrid tomatoes tend to exhibit a uniform appearance—smooth, round, and red. *Shutterstock*

On the other hand, heirloom tomatoes are found in a wide range of shapes, sizes, and colors. *Shutterstock*

Seeds and Seedlings Project

Test the efficacy of planting seedlings versus starting outdoors from seed with this fun project. Many types of vegetables have difficulty when transplanted, yet their lengthy growing time is better suited to an early start indoors. Start by planting seeds—pumpkin, for instance—directly into your garden as outlined in the seed package instructions. Then, transplant a seedling into your garden. At the end of the season, compare your results. Did the transplanted seedling thrive? Were the plants grown outdoors from seed less productive due to the longer amount of time they needed to get growing? Record your experiences for future reference.

Soil Preparation

You have your seeds or seedlings, and you have your garden area selected. Now what? Can you just stick them in the ground and hope for the best? Well, you could, but the success of your garden would be sorely affected. You'll want to work on soil preparation first.

Types of Soil

Soil gives plants somewhere to live, something to hold onto, and somewhere to search for water and find food. The type of soil you have will play a huge part in the success of your vegetable garden. Let's take a look at different types of soil and what effects they can have on your plants.

- Sandy soil requires a lot of watering. The loose texture of sand allows it to drain well. Good drainage is important for your garden, but if it's too good, the soil dries out far too quickly. Additionally, the soil can lose nutrients too quickly if they are washed away as the soil drains. Supplement sandy soil with heavier soil that's rich in organic matter.

- Clay soil is the opposite of sandy soil. It is heavy and retains water—too much, at times. Clay soil does not drain well and, consequently, it's not ideal for plants. It's also difficult to till. Supplement clay soil with organic matter.

- Loam soil is in between sandy and clay—a perfect balance. Most plants like a nice loamy soil, and it's easy to see why. Loamy soil is "fluffy"—full of organic matter, rich, and crumbly. It's hard to explain this type of soil, but once you've seen it, you'll never mistake it for anything else.

Here are two simple tests to determine whether you have sand, loam, or clay soil. The first is the simplest: dampen a small amount of your soil and try to roll it into a small ball. If your soil is sandy, your attempts to create a ball will fail—the soil will just keep

Is your soil sandy? Full of clay? Or a lovely, loose, loamy soil? Your soil type will play a large factor in how you prepare it for planting.

falling to bits. With soil that contains a lot of clay, the ball will form rather easily and retain its shape. If it's loam, the soil will form a ball, but will crumble and fall apart easily.

A slightly more elaborate soil test requires a clear glass jar, some water, and soil from your garden area. Fill the glass jar about halfway with the soil sample, then add water to about an inch from the top. Screw the top on tightly, and shake the jar vigorously for a couple of minutes.

Leave the jar to sit overnight. You should find that distinct layers form at the bottom of the jar. The sandy particles, being heaviest, will form the bottom layer, with clay on top. The layer in the middle is called silt. The thickness of each layer will give a fair approximation of your soil's content. If the bottom sandy layer is thicker than the other layers, you have sandy soil; likewise, a thick top clay layer represents plenty of clay in your garden. If you see a fairly even mixture of sand, silt, and clay, you have a nice loamy soil.

Tilling

If you are going to be using a garden space that has been worked in the recent past, then soil preparation may not be very difficult. On the other hand, if the space you have picked out has never been used for gardening before, then the job of soil preparation will be somewhat more challenging. In either case, you need to know where you stand before you can make any decisions. Take a shovel and push it in as far as it will go, and then turn that piece of ground over. Do this a few times in a few different spots. Take a look at the dirt. Is the soil stiff and hard? Plants won't grow very well in that type of soil, so something must be done. You need to work this soil around and add some organic matter to help make it soft and supple. There are a couple ways of doing this.

If you're starting a brand-new garden bed in a grassy location, the top layer of sod must be removed.

Tilling a garden by hand is an effective way to prepare your soil, especially if you're only utilizing a small space.

Tilling by hand

You can turn the soil yourself with simple garden tools like a shovel and fork. There are some advantages to this. You can remove weeds completely, roots and all. Rocks, too, can be discarded at this time. Stiff clumps can be raked or banged apart with a fork. The idea is to break up all the stiff areas and make the soil fresh and soft—so soft you can easily make footprints. (By the way, don't make footprints! If you walk over the area you just tilled, you'll squish the soil back down again.) If there is grass growing on the surface of your gardening site, you will want to remove it and its roots, but be sure to leave as much of the important topsoil as possible. (You can pick up individual pieces of turf and shake the soil out of their roots.) Because of the control you have in removing weeds and because you will be able to get down nice and deep, tilling by hand is a good idea—especially if your garden area is not particularly large.

Tilling with a machine

A machine can do a fine, quick job of soil preparation, but it may lead to other issues. For instance, you may need help in either acquiring or operating the machine. Rototillers can be dangerous if used improperly. Also, a rototiller may not be able to dig down as deeply as you need (although that's not to say you couldn't use the machine first and go back over the area by hand later). Any weeds in the area get chopped up rather than being removed and could reappear later on, causing a weedier garden than you might have had with a hand-tilled garden. Rototillers don't like rocks very much, so you have to be careful not to hit too many.

That said, it is almost certainly faster and easier to use a rototiller—and for large gardens, you may not have a choice because going over the entire area by hand will simply take too long.

Our advice: If your garden is small, don't bother with a machine. If your garden is large, or you have easy access to a machine (and help to run it) go for it.

If you're utilizing raised beds, you're adding fresh soil, so tilling is not necessary.

No-till method

You can also investigate the "no-till" method of gardening, which is gaining in popularity.

The no-till method has its advantages (such as reduced watering and fewer weeds and less hard labor), but it requires you to plan ahead. Start months before your projected planting date (ideally the autumn before). Place several layers of newspaper or cardboard on top of your garden area (no need to remove the sod first). Wet those layers thoroughly, and then add a few inches of hay, straw, grass clippings, wood shavings, or leaves. Wet that layer, and top it off with a layer of compost. Leave these layers to settle until spring, at which time you can start planting. The benefits of no-till gardening are definitely worth the effort, but it's not a method that you can use at the spur of the moment, so plan in advance.

Machine tilling is particularly helpful if your garden is large. Always exercise caution when operating this type of machine—wearing heavy gloves and goggles is highly recommended.

Testing the Soil

If your soil is extremely acidic or alkaline, you'll need to amend it before trying to grow a vegetable garden. How do you know if your soil is acidic, alkaline, or neutral? Have it tested.

Your local agricultural extension service can help you with soil testing. You provide a soil sample, and they provide you with a detailed analysis of the soil's components. Or you can invest in a digital meter that measures the pH of your garden's soil. For between $20 and $35, you can purchase one of these handy devices, which will tell you if your soil is acidic, alkaline, or neutral. Then you can compensate by adding the proper nutrients to balance the soil's pH. Soil that's too acidic can be treated with lime, and sulfur will help lower the pH of alkaline soil.

Understanding Soil pH

	MODERATELY ACIDIC	SLIGHTLY ACIDIC	NEUTRAL	SLIGHTLY ALKALINE
pH	4.5–5.9	6.0–6.9	7.0	7.1–8.0

The pH preferences of each vegetable are listed in the vegetable profiles in Chapter 5. If your soil falls in the 6.0 to 8.0 range, you should have little difficulty is growing most types of vegetables and probably won't need to adjust the pH. The majority of vegetables are very adaptable to this range of soil pH. Even more important than pH is the overall condition of your soil and its nutrient content.

However, there are a few vegetables and fruits (notably potatoes and blueberries) that do much better when the soil is under 6.0.

Adding Nutrients

Fertilizers are an excellent source of three essential nutrients: nitrogen, phosphorus, and potassium. These nutrients together are commonly referred to as NPK. (N stands for nitrogen, P stands for phosphorus, and K stands for potassium—and no, it doesn't make sense, unless you have a close working relationship with the periodic table of the elements.) The numbers on the fertilizer bags represent the percentage by weight that it contains of each nutrient, such as 10-10-10, which translates to 10 percent nitrogen, 10 percent phosphorus, and 10 percent potassium.

Organic and inorganic (or synthetic) fertilizers deliver the same content (nitrogen, phosphorus, and potassium), but their origin and their impact on the soil differs greatly. Organic fertilizer comes from natural sources (plants or animals) and synthetic fertilizer is manufactured. Synthetic fertilizers work very quickly, but they don't add any organic matter, which is the stuff that makes your soil rich and fluffy. Many people prefer to use organic fertilizer (such as composted manure or compost made from kitchen scraps and garden debris). We always use organic fertilizer. Thanks to our horses and rabbits, we have an ample supply of quality compost that helps improve our garden soil. It also allows us to pursue organic gardening, which has added environmental benefits. It's rewarding to munch on veggies that you know were grown in organic soil.

The Basics of Manure

If you live on a farm or in a rural area where ample supplies of manure are available, you may want to take a pile of manure and turn it into composted fertilizer. It isn't hard at all; let's explore your options.

Horse. Horse manure is widely available from horse owners, although typically you can't buy it commercially. It must be thoroughly composted as it is a "hot" manure that will burn plants if not decomposed long enough.

Poultry. Another "hot" manure—slightly higher in nitrogen than horse or cow manure.

You'll want to be sure to add the proper amendments to optimize your soil's potential. For instance, when planting potatoes, you might have to add sulfur to make the soil sufficiently acidic.

Cow. This is most likely what you will find at your local garden center. Although it isn't as nutrient-rich as some of the other types, it is easy to obtain, especially if you don't live in a rural area with other options.

Goat and Sheep. These are well-liked because they are "tidier" types of manure than cow, horse, or poultry. Goat and sheep manure comes in a convenient "pelleted" form, which leads some people to attempt spreading the manure prior to composting; however, this is not recommended. It's always better to compost first.

Rabbit. Considered by many to be nature's ideal fertilizer, rabbit manure contains high amounts of nitrogen and phosphorus, more than any of the other manure types mentioned. Again, beware of the temptation to spread prior to composting. Wait and let it rot.

Making Your Own Compost

Okay, you've been given two wheelbarrow loads of rabbit manure and you'd like to try composting it. What's the first step?

Examples of Soil-utions for Common Problems

PROBLEM	SOIL MIGHT NEED	POSSIBLE SOURCES
Your plants have weak stems, yellowish leaves, and poor root growth.	*Potassium* to help plants process nutrients and water	Kelp meal, potash, woodash
Your plants are not growing or producing well.	*Phosphorous* to aid in photosynthesis and growth	Bone meal, rock phosphate
Soil testing has revealed that your soil is too acidic.	*Nitrogen* to raise the pH of the soil	Lime, woodash
Soil testing has revealed that your soil is too alkaline.	*Sulfur* to lower the pH of the soil	Elemental sulfur, ammonium nitrate, urea
Your plants are not growing well, have strangely shaped leaves or leaves with brown spots, or have developed blossom end rot on the fruit.	*Calcium* to increase plant growth and production	Lime (if soil is acidic) Eggshells, calcium tablets, gypsum (if soil is alkaline)
Your plants are growing slowly and are developing yellowed leaves.	*Magnesium, nitrogen*	Epsom salts, limestone

> **TIP**
>
> Fertilizers are an excellent source of three essential nutrients: nitrogen, phosphorus, and potassium. These nutrients together are commonly referred to as NPK.

You can purchase bags of compost from your local garden center, or you can make compost yourself, either from manure or from kitchen scraps and garden debris.

Begin by deciding if you'll prepare an official compost bin or if you'll settle for a compost heap. There are varying types of compost bins, including prefabricated bins that are similar in appearance to large outdoor plastic garbage cans but with air vents and no bottoms. Many municipalities provide city-sanctioned compost bins to residents at a low cost. You can also make your own compost bin using wooden pallets or a combination of wire and wood. A compost heap is less formal; basically, it's an open pile of compost wherever you choose to put it. Keep in mind that if you live in an urban or suburban area, official compost bins may be

If you raise livestock, then you have a ready supply of manure that will be excellent for making compost.

required for composting projects. In either case, be sure that you select an appropriate place for your composting project: out of the way, out of sight, and out of—yes—smell.

A common size for a compost bin is 3 × 3 × 3 feet, but you can adjust this size to meet your own particular needs.

Locate some organic material. Dried leaves work well, as do hay and straw. Fresh grass clippings are another excellent choice. Leftovers from your kitchen—including eggshells, coffee grounds, and vegetable peelings—work well, as all of these are excellent organic material.

Now, place a quantity of fresh manure on your compost bin or in your compost heap. Add a portion of the organic hay/grass mixture, and mix both piles together thoroughly. Add more manure, then more organic material. Let it sit. Come back every few days and stir it around, adding more material on a regular basis. If your compost appears too dry, try adding water, but if your compost begins to smell very bad, the mixture may be too wet. Add no further water until it has a chance

to dry out and the smell subsides. A bad smell can also indicate the presence of too much nitrogen; in this case you might add some additional dry leaves to help reduce the percentage of nitrogen.

The composting process varies in length depending on the type of manure used, but count on needing at least sixty days, and don't be surprised if you need more.

Finished compost should be dark and crumbly (some say it should resemble the consistency of chocolate cake) and not smelly. Late in the season, in the fall after harvest, is an excellent time to add compost to your garden soil. Work it in thoroughly and then let it sit over the winter.

Planting

Find out the average date of the last frost in your area. Circle this date in red on your calendar. While this date is not a foolproof way of deciding when it's safe to

No-No's of Composting

- Do not use dog or cat manure in your compost bin. These can contain harmful parasites and diseases.

- Always compost manure thoroughly. Do not use fresh manure in your garden or it will "burn" and potentially kill your plants. The process of composting produces heat, which kills the bacteria in the manure, so in order to avoid potential harm do not use manure until the composting process is completely finished.

- When adding kitchen scraps, avoid fatty, greasy, oily foods. These may attract rodents, which is not something you wish to encourage. Also, do not add meat scraps to your compost bin. Stick with veggie and fruit scraps, coffee and tea grounds, and eggshells.

A wheelbarrow full of manure isn't easy to move around, but it is a wonderful and beneficial addition to your compost pile.

All About Manure Tea

Yes, it sounds disgusting. It's hard to imagine where such a delectable name originated, but it probably came from the fact that manure tea is considered to be the ideal "drink" for your nutrient-thirsty garden. Here's how to "brew" this concoction.

You will need:

- A shovelful of composted manure (don't use fresh manure for this project)
- A large bucket
- Warm water—enough to fill the bucket

Place the manure in the bottom of the bucket, and then slowly add the warm water until the water level reaches near the top of the bucket. Now, go away and leave it alone for a few hours. Then remove some of the "manure tea" liquid and place it in a small container, which you can add to your plants as necessary.

plant, it is helpful in getting a ballpark idea of planting time. Your tender seedlings will definitely have to wait until the last date of frost has passed, but you can begin working on some of your early spring "cold crops," such as peas, radishes, and lettuce. Count backward about two weeks prior to the date circled on your calendar, and sow your cold crop seeds at that point. (See "Frosty Worries" on page 55 for a complete list of cold crops.)

If you're starting your seeds in outdoor rows, as you likely will be if you're planting carrots or lettuce or beans, mark the anticipated place for your row (make sure it's straight!). Then it's time to make your holes. There are a lot of ways to make your holes, but our favorite method is to take a bamboo stake that is about half an inch in diameter. Then we take an ordinary wooden clothespin (the kind with a metal spring) and snap it on to the stake. Attach the clothespin at whatever depth you plan to plant your seeds. For instance, if you're planting beans, and you'd like to plant them 1 inch deep, attach the clothespin 1 inch from the bottom of the stake. Then press the bamboo stake into the ground until it reaches the clothespin, and you'll make precise 1-inch holes every time.

This compost pile is contained by a wire mesh fence. The pile contains a nice combination of leaves, grass clippings, and other garden debris.

Planting in rows is the standard when sowing many types of vegetables, including carrots, corn, and onions.

If you're looking for a handy way to measure the depth of your holes for planting, place a clothespin on the end of a bamboo stick at precisely the depth you need...

...and press the bamboo stake into the ground until the clothespin meets the ground. This ensures that the hole is exactly the depth desired, and you can adjust the clothespin as necessary.

When planting seedlings, be sure to press gently but firmly on the soil around the base of the plant.

For transplanting seedlings, you'll need to get out your trowel and dig some holes. Always dig the hole larger than the size of the transplant's roots and set it in the hole. Then fill in the gaps with soil and press gently but firmly to eliminate any pockets of air. Water lightly and be sure to mark the seedling with a small card or stake (or keep a garden journal). Don't assume that you'll remember which seedlings are which—you won't.

If you'd like to try something different from the traditional garden rows, you might consider square foot gardening. Popularized by Mel Bartholomew's bestselling book, *The Square Foot Garden*, this method involves square-shaped raised beds. Instead of planting in long rows, you plant in small square boxes. The method takes up less space, making it a good choice if your gardening space is very limited.

Making Hills

Lots of vegetables like to grow in hills. Most types of summer and winter squash, cucumbers, and pumpkins all do well when planted in hills; this allows for excellent root growth and the absorption of nutrients.

Hills are easy to make—and kind of fun, too. A hill is simply a raised heap of soil, approximately 12 to 24 inches in diameter and 4 to 8 inches in height. Select the location in your garden where you'd like to position your hills, and start bringing the soil together with your hands. Once you've made your hills, make four to six evenly spaced holes in each hill. These holes are where your seeds will go. You'll likely need to thin your seedlings later on, depending on which vegetable you've planted in your hills.

Trellising

You've planted your seeds or seedlings, but that doesn't mean your job is done. Some of them will need your help in order to thrive. Some vegetables—such as pole beans and most varieties of peas—require a bit of an extra hand, in the form of staking or trellising.

There are many different ways to build a trellis—you can fashion one from bamboo stakes (the tipi type is simple and only requires three bamboo sticks), or you can let your vegetables climb up a fence, or you can build a trellis with wood.

Some plants don't require a full trellis but could use a bit of extra support. For your tender seedlings (tomatoes and peppers, particularly), you can use short, 12-inch bamboo stakes to prevent them from being tossed about in the wind. You'll want to provide tall stakes or large cages for your tomatoes once the plants have begun to grow and expand. Using the vertical space of your garden gives you more room, and the produce is often healthier and cleaner when it is kept off the ground.

Squash, cucumbers, and pumpkins are among the vegetables often planted in hills. *Shutterstock*

Tomato cages are useful for supporting your tomato plants, particularly the indeterminate varieties. These small seedlings can also benefit from the protection of the cages, as windy conditions can cause harm to tender seedlings.

There are many different types of trellising and staking—feel free to experiment to see what works best for your situation.

Multiple-Planting Methods

Double-cropping

If you plant a fast-maturing vegetable (such as peas) early in the spring, you'll discover that they are just about finished in early to midsummer. Then what? Does that space in your garden simply go to waste for the remainder of the season? Never fear, double-cropping is here. When your peas have finished producing, simply pull up the plants, work the soil a bit, and start again. This time, plant a vegetable that thrives on warm summer weather, such as summer squash. By continuing to plant your garden space, you've effectively doubled your crop yield without needing any additional garden space. Double-cropping works exceptionally well in areas with long growing seasons, but can also be achieved if your growing season is short.

Succession planting

A variation on double-cropping is succession planting. Let's say that you love fresh green beans and you want to eat them for the entire summer. To be sure that you'll have plenty of green beans all season long, continue to plant them every couple of weeks for the duration of the summer. As one planting matures and stops producing, your next crop will be coming along.

Lettuce is a quick-growing crop, so it is a good candidate for succession planting or double-cropping when planted early in spring.

Intercropping

This is one of our favorite ways to increase the production of a garden. Intercropping involves planting more than one crop in a particular area. For instance, this year we planted single rows of carrots in between our tomato plants, thus minimizing the need for additional space reserved especially for carrots.

Frosty Worries

Let's say that it's late May and your entire garden is now safely in the ground. You've planted your seeds, transplanted your seedlings, and everything appears to be going well. But what if the weather forecast predicts a frost—or even worse, a hard freeze? What of your tender vegetation? Some of your plants will probably fare perfectly well—the ones that are tolerant of frost or freezing temperatures. These frost-hardy vegetables include root crops such as beets, carrots, parsnips, potatoes, radishes, and turnips. (Sweet potatoes, however, are not frost-hardy). Other hardy crops include members of the cabbage family, including Brussels sprouts, kohlrabi, collards, kale, mustard greens, broccoli, Chinese cabbage, Chinese broccoli, cauliflower, and cabbage itself. All of these are hardy or semi-hardy. Additionally, peas, spinach, celery, and lettuce are also fairly hardy and can withstand cold temperatures.

The vegetables that you'll have to be especially careful of are tomatoes, peppers, corn, and beans. Also be careful of vine plants such as cucumber, pumpkin, and squash, as well as eggplants and sweet potatoes; they do not tolerate cold temperatures.

You'll want to protect these sensitive plants from the frost. There are several ways you can accomplish this. Plastic tarps (especially dark ones) are helpful for protecting a large number of plants at one time. You can also try sheets or blankets, or you can cover your plants individually by using garbage bags, glass cloches, or buckets. Always take care not to damage the foliage of your tender young plants with the covering. If you have cold frames, these also work well.

In autumn, it is devastating to lose your hard work to an early, out-of-season frost or freeze. For the frost-sensitive plants, you can either try to cover them as discussed previously, or you can try to harvest the produce early. Salvaging as much produce as you can is preferable to losing an entire crop, but remember that if you're able to assist your plants in withstanding the frost, you might have several more weeks of frost-free weather before cold temperatures come your way again. In this respect, it's wise to leave as many young vegetables on the plants as you can to give them the opportunity to obtain additional growing time—as long as you're able to nurse the plants through the cold snap.

Make Your Own String Trellis

If you are growing peas or pole beans, you'll notice pretty quickly that the plants want to move around and go somewhere. They're not at all satisfied in hanging out on the ground. It's as if the plant looks around and says, "Hey, this is boring—let's go somewhere!" It's up to you to give the plants something sturdy to grow on.

A string trellis is a very simple trellis to make for lightweight plants such as peas. There are other methods of trellising that are more elaborate, but foryour first experiment with trellising, this is a fun andeasy way.

You'll need a few sticks or poles about five feet long; bamboo stakes work well. You'll also need some kind of twine or wire; kite string can work and is inexpensive. Push the sticks into the ground, one at each end of each row. Then, using the string, tie a taut line between the two poles, a few inches off the ground. Be careful not to let the strings hang loosely. Tie more taut lines between the poles, each line a few inches higher than the other, until you have something that looks like the trellis below.

Now comes the fun part. Slowly and carefully, your climbing plants will start to explore the strings. It's truly fascinating to watch them send out their viney fingers (called "tendrils") and literally grab hold of the strings and pull themselves up. This will happen as quickly as a few days, and once the vines have a firm hold of the strings, they will climb faster.

The Three Sisters Method

Native Americans introduced the "Three Sisters" method of planting vegetables. Corn, beans, and squash are planted together, with the tall corn providing a place for the pole beans to climb, and the squash nestling on the ground underneath the corn and bean plants. Some say that the presence of the squash plants deters raccoons from going after your ears of corn; raccoons don't like stepping on the prickly squash leaves. These complementary crops grow very well together and represent a time-tested method of "companion planting." Enjoy a bit of gardening heritage and give the Three Sisters method a try!

A very sad sight! This tomato plant has been damaged by an early autumn frost.

These tomato plants and cages have been protected by black plastic. The plastic protected the plants from an early frost, and the plants were able to keep producing for a few more weeks.

The Growing Season, Beginning to End

Starting onions from plants is an easy way to get a jumpstart on the growing season. Planting is easy, so water them regularly and then stand back and watch 'em grow! It doesn't take long before they are well on their way, and by the end of summer you'll be happily harvesting handfuls of mature onions. Share them with your friends!

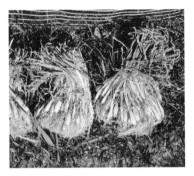
Onion seedlings, ready to plant

Planting a row of onions

Onion patch just planted

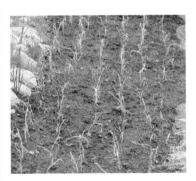
Onion patch after one week

Onion patch at six weeks

Onion patch at two months

Harvesting onions after about three months

Flowers in Your Garden

Don't forget about flowers! You'll want to leave some space in and around your garden for this purpose. There are several reasons flowers make a great addition to a vegetable garden. They're pretty, fun, easy to grow, and satisfying to have around. But there are practical reasons, too. Some flowers, like marigolds, are natural bug repellents, discouraging whiteflies, hornworms, and other pests.

The best reason to grow flowers in your vegetable garden is that they attract bees. Some of your vegetable plants are wind pollinated, but others require bees for pollination. No bees, no vegetables (or, few bees, few vegetables). Almost all vegetables require pollination in order to grow "fruits": tomatoes, peas, beans, all kinds of squash, and the list goes on. (Vegetables we can harvest without help from the bees include root crops like carrots and radishes and leaf crops like lettuce. This is because we don't eat these plants' fruit.) The more flowers you plant, the more bees will be attracted to your garden. And while they're examining your flowers, the bees will almost certainly stop over by the vegetable part of the garden and see what's going on there. You might also consider the possibility of keeping a hive or two of bees; this will undoubtedly help increase the number of bees that visit your garden.

You can fill the spaces between your rows with flowers, or you can plant the perimeter of your garden with flowers, or you could plant some large flowering bushes in each corner. Just be careful not to let your flowers shade your vegetables. The possibilities are endless; by enticing bees into your vegetable garden, you'll reap dividends.

Chapter 4

Daily Garden Care

Your garden depends on you for care and attention. You may decide not to work in your garden every single day, but you must tend to regular chores in order to keep your garden healthy and productive. In this chapter, we'll discuss watering, weeding, thinning, and mulching, as well as problems that you may encounter in your garden: diseases and pests (both insects and critters).

Watering

Before you rush out with a hose and flood your garden under a deluge of water, take a moment to consider this: Water is important to a garden, but too much is as harmful as not enough. Aim for a happy medium.

A good rule of thumb is to aim for one inch of water per week, more in extreme heat. If your area has been receiving plenty of rain, then you'll need to water your garden far less than you would if your area were experiencing a drought.

Some vegetables require more water than others do; for instance, cauliflower requires ample water, much more than other vegetables.

Keep an eye on your plants. If it's a very hot day (or a few hot days in a row), your plants will need more watering than they do when the weather is cool. If your plants are looking a bit wilted, give them a drink, even if it's not your regularly scheduled watering day.

When you water your vegetables, try to avoid getting water on the leaves late in the day, when they won't dry quickly. Wet leaves encourage the spread of powdery

Watering your garden is one of the most important things you can do to promote a successful vegetable crop.

mildew and other plant diseases. We think that a system of soaker hoses is the best way to water your garden—the water is deposited at the base of the plant, so the leaves don't get wet. If you can't set up a system of soaker hoses, we'd suggest watering the garden with a watering can or a hose with a spray nozzle, both of which allow you to water at ground level. If you don't have the time to water the garden by hand, you'll need a sprinkler. If you use a sprinkler, try to water early in the morning (as early as possible). Early is better for two reasons: water gets a chance to soak into the ground rather than evaporate under the midday sun, and the leaves get a chance to dry out before evening. Try not to work in the garden when the leaves are wet, as this can spread disease.

Weeding

Sooner or later, your garden is going to be infested with weeds. All of the qualities that make your garden desirable for vegetables (fertile soil, ample water, sunlight) also make it desirable for weeds. Weeds are troublesome because they compete with your plants for the nutrients and water in the soil. They can also crowd your growing seedlings. In addition, weeds aren't usually considered to be attractive additions to your garden.

The best way to prevent your garden from becoming a jungle is to clear away any unwanted weed growth before the job becomes too big. One method is to use a hoe to lightly rake the soil in between rows once a week. Be sure not to stray too close to any stems, and not to dig so deep that you disturb the roots of your vegetables. For areas quite close to plants you care about, it's best to carefully pull out those weeds by hand.

Isn't it funny? We can spend all this time and effort persuading useful plants to grow, and they sometimes seem to fight every effort, while the lucky weeds just dive in and take off growing without a second thought—and without anyone nurturing them a bit. The weeds get stepped on, crushed, run over with the hose, hit with the shovel, and pulled off at the stem,

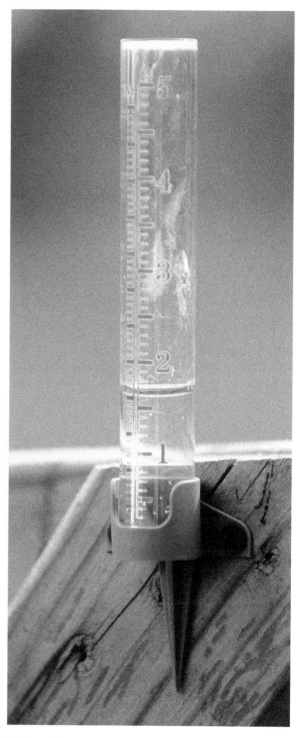

Not sure how much water your garden is receiving? Place a rain gauge in your garden and you'll know exactly how much rain has fallen.

but they never stop growing. Nobody waters them (at least, not on purpose), but the weeds don't care. They just grow.

If you keep destroying weeds and they just keep coming back, you might not be removing all of the root system. Make sure you hang on tight and pull straight up to ensure the entire root is removed. A regular weeding schedule (ten minutes a day or twenty to thirty minutes every two days) will keep things under control nicely.

People tend to overestimate the amount of time involved in the weeding process. Whenever we mention to someone that we are putting in our annual vegetable garden, they inevitably reply: "Oh, my. I suppose it takes a lot of time to do the weeding."

The truth of it is that weeding is the least of our worries. Certainly it takes time, but it occurs after you've already devoted hours and hours to all of the other aspects of gardening: preparing the soil, starting the seeds, selecting seedlings, transplanting seedlings, mulching, watering, staking, trellising, and the list goes on. Weeding is just another part of the package, but it's certainly not a task that overpowers all of the others.

Thinning

It might seem awful to think about after all your careful nurturing, but in some cases it will be necessary for you to thin out your rows by removing some of the seedlings. The reason for this is to give the remaining plants enough room to grow happily. Take carrots, for instance. Chances are your sprouts will pop up all nice and healthy, ready to grow—and way too close together. If you were to leave all of the sprouts to themselves, at harvest time you would find that very few of the carrots had matured into good-size produce because they were squeezing each other all summer and preventing each other from having adequate room to grow. The same thing can happen to radishes, beets, turnips, corn, and many other vegetables.

When you do thin, be careful not to disturb the roots or stalks of the seedlings that you've chosen to leave in the garden. Take hold of the seedling and pull straight up, the same way you would remove a weed, or cut off the extra plants at the base, using manicure scissors.

Will you be spending all of your spare time pulling weeds in your garden? Not if you take some time each day to keep the weed population under control.

Root vegetables, like the carrots shown here, require thinning from time to time. If not thinned, the carrots will not grow properly.

Dry grass clippings make an excellent mulch. Spread the clippings around your small plants to keep moisture in the ground and to reduce weeds.

The Magic of Mulching

It's time for a shout-out to the merits of mulching. A light layer of mulch (straw, hay, wood shavings, or grass clippings) nestled around your seedlings can work wonders for keeping weeds at bay, as well as helping the ground retain moisture. The mulching is also helpful to increase the fertility of your soil. Grass clippings in particular add many nutrients to the soil.

A few notes of caution: Don't add mulch too early. Never add mulch before the seeds have sprouted or when the seedlings are still tiny and the soil is still cool. Withhold the mulch until they are taller, at least 3 or 4 inches. Keep the mulch away from the base of each plant.

Additional Fertilizing

Most of the time, you'll be adding your composted manure or fertilizer to your garden soil long before planting your seeds or seedlings, preferably in the late fall after harvest. However, there is another type of supplemental fertilizing known as "side dressing" or "topdressing." This involves adding additional fertilizer to the top of the soil and nestling it around your plants during the growing season, when the original nutrient sources have been depleted. You don't work side-dressed fertilizer into the soil; it's simply left on the top to be absorbed. This provides necessary additional nutrients for your growing plants.

TIP

A light layer of mulch (straw, hay, wood shavings, or grass clippings) nestled around your seedlings can work wonders for keeping weeds at bay, as well as helping the ground retain moisture.

DISEASE	TYPE	SYMPTOMS	PREVENTION/TREATMENT
Fusarium wilt	Fungus	Yellow, wilting leaves	Remove infected plants
Scab	Bacteria	Scabby areas	Crop rotation
Powdery mildew	Fungus	Dusty, powder-like coating on leaves	Good air circulation, avoid wet leaves
Verticillium wilt	Fungus	Yellow spots on leaves	Crop rotation
Bacterial wilt	Bacteria	Wilting leaves	Remove infected plants, control of cucumber beetle
Leaf blights	Bacteria/fungus	Spots and browning of leaves	Air circulation, avoid wet leaves, remove infected plants
Bulb rot	Bacteria/fungus	Rotted ends of bulbs	Air circulation, avoid wet leaves, removed infected plants
Virus diseases (mosaic)	Virus	Mottled, yellowed leaves	Choose resistant varieties if available; remove infected plants
Blossom end rot	Calcium deficiency	Rotted area on fruit	Maintain moisture equilibrium

Allowing ample space between plants makes them less vulnerable to disease.

You might want to encourage some pests. Here, a trio of black swallowtail caterpillars devours a dill plant, but they'll pay the garden back by turning into beautiful butterflies.

Potential Garden Problems

As if it weren't enough to be fighting the weather and weeds for your garden's success, there are several other adversaries that can also wreak havoc with your garden: diseases, insects, and critters.

Plant Diseases

Unfortunately, there are a number of diseases that can affect your vegetable plants, inhibiting growth and production and ruining produce. Here are some of the most common plant diseases:

So, what can you do to keep your garden healthy? The best thing to do is make note of any problems and plan ahead to next year. Crop rotation is a good strategy,

as discussed in Chapter 1. If your squash is overtaken by powdery mildew, do not plant squash in the same location next year, and avoid planting vegetables that are susceptible to powdery mildew in that particular location. It's also important to remove all plant debris at the end of the growing season.

Another strategy is to allow plenty of space between plants. Don't overplant any particular area, as this can increase the incidence of plant disease. Ample space allows good airflow between each plant. This will vary from plant to plant, as the definition of "ample space"

Birds can help reduce the number of insect pests in your garden, so welcome them with berry bushes and fruit trees.

between bean plants and "ample space" between winter squash plants is vastly different.

You can also increase your chances of raising healthy plants by selecting disease-resistant varieties. For instance, if you're having trouble with verticillium wilt on your tomatoes, then try planting varieties that are resistant to verticillium wilt (indicated by a "V" after the name of the variety).

Insects

Insects are a normal part of the average garden— some of them are even beneficial. There are instances, however, when they cause trouble. Thankfully, there are many things that you can do to prevent or minimize damage from insects.

Birds. It can be helpful to have birds frequenting your garden; they love to feast on insects and they are a naturally efficient way to reduce your

Set up birdhouses and birdbaths to encourage birds to visit your garden.

insect population. Entice birds to your garden by providing bird-friendly habitat. Set up birdhouses and a birdbath, and make your garden as pleasant as possible for the birds you wish to attract.

Crop rotation. At planting time each spring, rearrange your vegetables so that they are planted in different locations from the previous year. This is beneficial in more ways than one, but it is particularly helpful in avoiding insect trouble. This technique is most effective in large gardens.

Water works! Spraying your vegetable plant forcefully with a hose can be a very effective way of reducing the number of insect pests in your garden. Do this only as necessary, when numerous pests (such as aphids) have been sighted. Spraying the leaves of a vegetable plant is not an ideal measure, but you must weigh the pros and cons of having a pest-filled garden versus the possibility of damaging your plants with the water spray.

Got chickens? Chickens like to munch on insects, so if your wild bird population isn't doing the trick, you might try giving chickens access to your garden for a limited period of time. Don't leave the chickens in there for long, though, as they will happily eat the vegetable plants, too.

The bottom line is there are many options for reducing pests in your garden without resorting to chemical sprays or poisons. Those should truly be your last resort and are almost always unnecessary measures for home gardens. One of the delights of raising your own vegetables is that you have the reassurance that your produce is not covered

Organic or Not?

If you're interested in growing vegetables organically but aren't sure if they will grow as well without the aid of chemical fertilizers and pesticides, try an experiment. Prepare two garden beds (keep them a good distance apart), and plant them with the same variety of vegetable. In the first bed, use only organic fertilizers and natural forms of pest repellents. In the second bed, go ahead and use chemical fertilizer and other chemical products as necessary. At the end of the season, compare the results. Which garden bed produced the most vegetables? Was there any difference in the quality or condition of the vegetables? Did either have a higher incidence of pest damage? Record your findings. Did the results surprise you or were they what you expected?

iStockphoto.com/Steve Froehe

Ground squirrels can wreak havoc on your vegetable garden. They are especially fond of leaf lettuce and tomatoes, but they don't mind taking bites out of squash or cucumbers and will eat all the peas!

with pesticides. A method called integrated pest management (IPM) has become the standard in recent years—it recommends the use of sprays or poisons only in extreme circumstances after all other methods of pest removal have been exhausted. If a vegetable is a problem year after year, just don't plant it.

Critters

Cute though they may be, wildlife can be disastrous to your garden.

Deer are beautiful visitors but hazardous to your vegetable garden. If they are frequenting your garden, you may need to invest in a tall (at least 6-foot-high) fence. Now, having said that, we understand that erecting a tall fence is not a cheap, quick, or easy solution. We have personally had some success with a lower fence; the visual appearance of the fence deters all but the most persistent of deer, and it was extremely simple to set up and not expensive.

Ground squirrels (also known as gophers, depending on your locale) are troublesome creatures:

These burrowing critters dig numerous holes in your garden, they steal tomatoes, they take bites out of zucchini squash, they pluck peapods from the vine, and they help themselves to the choicest pieces of heirloom leaf lettuce. In short, they are naughty, naughty, naughty. The average fence is ineffective at keeping squirrels out of the garden. The little critters either climb over it or dig under it, or if all else fails, squeeze themselves through the smallest of openings.

Rabbits are not quite as troublesome as squirrels, but they still perform their fair share of naughtiness. You can usually keep the rabbits out of your garden with a 30-inch-high wire mesh fence. Most of the time they aren't persistent enough to dig under the fence, and they're not agile enough to leap a fence that high.

Birds aren't as much of a threat as some of the other critters; in fact, they can be helpful in reducing insects in your garden. You might find a few beak marks in a tomato

Look out for your carrots! Actually, rabbits will probably leave your carrots alone, since they will be too busy devouring your green beans. Fencing may be necessary to keep these critters out of your garden.

here and there, but that's about the extent of most bird trouble. The exception? Crows can cause trouble in your corn field, and birds will eat the berries off your bushes.

Raccoons, like crows, love to eat ripe corn. To avoid this scenario, harvest your ears of corn as soon as they are ready—don't wait around.

There are lots of old wives' tales for keeping critters out of your garden; you can try any and all of them if you so desire. These ideas include putting up scarecrows, keeping a radio on in the garden at night, hanging bags of human hair around the perimeter of your garden, placing helium balloons around your garden, and so on. You may find that the ideas work well, or don't work at all. The evidence of success is anecdotal at best, but if you find that something works, why not keep it up?

Garden beds with screened tops can be a very effective way to keep critters from dining on your low-growing vegetables or strawberries.

Making a Scarecrow

Whether or not you believe in the efficacy of scarecrows at keeping critters away, there's still a perfectly legitimate reason for keeping one in your garden: Because it's fun.

Scarecrows are easy to make because there are no hard and fast rules regarding their appearance or design. You can make a traditional scarecrow (à la *The Wizard of Oz*) wearing a plaid shirt stuffed with straw and a pair of torn jeans, or you can be original and make a scarecrow out of pumpkins or tires or an old sheet. Whatever you decide, remember the main rule of scarecrow building: Have fun!

Put your creative skills to work and create a scarecrow or two for your garden.

Chapter 5

All About Vegetables

This chapter introduces you to a wide variety of the most common vegetables. For each vegetable, we've included information on the necessary garden requirements, as well as planting information and special considerations that you should keep in mind. Also included is the estimated growing time for each vegetable as well as the proper soil pH for ideal growth.

Asparagus

If you're looking for a vegetable that will more than amply give back for the effort that you put in, consider growing asparagus. Your one-time planting of asparagus could conceivably continue producing for twenty years, and it's a popular sale item at farmers' markets, so you might be able to glean a bit of income from it as well.

Types: Most varieties are green, although you can find purple as well. Mary Washington is a well-known variety; look also for the newer Mary Washington Improved variety.

Garden Requirements: Sunshine is a must-have, but you'll also want to be sure that you plant your asparagus in a nice type of sandy loam soil with good drainage. You might consider devoting one garden bed entirely to asparagus, as its height can shade other plants and prevent them from gaining the benefits of full sun. Because asparagus is a perennial, you will want to select a suitable permanent place for your asparagus. Most are hardy in Zones 3 to 8; some gardeners have had success growing asparagus in Zone 2.

Edible stalks of asparagus. *Shutterstock*

Asparagus crowns.
iStockphoto.com/
Stefan Clapczynski

Special Considerations: Because it is a perennial, you must have plenty of manure worked into the soil before planting, as you won't be able to till and replenish your soil later on. Asparagus can be grown from seed, but purchasing "crowns" (one-year-old roots) is much more common. Two-year-old plants are also available at a higher price; three-year-old plants are priced higher still.

Planting Information: Plant your crowns in wide trenches, between 6 and 12 inches deep, and over 12 inches wide. Make mounds of compost in the trench, approximately 16 to 18 inches apart, then drape the crown over the top of the mound and cover with a couple of inches of soil. Add more soil on top as the plant grows, until the trench is eventually filled. Alternately, you can forego the trenching and simply plant in rows, 4 to 5 inches deep for crowns.

Growing Time: Three years. No, this is not a typographical error. Asparagus is a perennial plant that typically requires three years of growing before it produces a sizeable harvest. You can shorten this timeframe by purchasing two- or three-year-old crowns to speed things up.

Soil pH: Ideally 7.0 (neutral), but a range of 6.0 to 8.0 is acceptable.

Beans

The wonderful green bean is a staple in most gardens. And why not? Beans are easy to grow, they produce well, and they are delicious in a wide variety of recipes. And with myriad varieties and types, there is plenty of opportunity to experiment and have fun.

Types: Pole and bush beans are the two main classifications; within these two groups are numerous varieties. Our favorite bush variety is Empress; we love it for its abundant production and incredible taste. A fun pole variety is the Lazy Housewife. Unfortunately it produced for us exactly as its name implied: lazily. For a bit of color, plant Royalty Purple Pod, and if you want an exciting choice for dried beans, try Calypso.

Garden Requirements: Beans prefer to be planted in full sun and perform best in well-drained soil.

Special Considerations: Pole beans need the support of a trellis, fence, or poles to climb. Bush beans do not require these supports; they produce more abundantly but for a shorter time. Pole beans produce for a longer period of time, especially if you continually harvest the beans.

Planting Information: Beans should be planted well after the danger of frost is past. Do not plant your beans too early; frost is very dangerous to beans. Bush beans are somewhat hardier than pole beans, so you can safely plant bush beans after the *average* last frost date has passed; wait another two weeks or so until the latest possible frost date has passed before planting pole beans. Plant your seeds 1 to 1½ inches deep, and place two seeds per hole. Make your holes 2 to 4 inches apart, and space your rows 2 to 3 feet apart.

Beans.

Growing Time: 50 to 90 days, depending on the variety. Bush beans are the quickest; pole, lima, and soy beans require more time. For your bush beans, if you wish to eat them as fresh snap beans, the maturity date is faster. If you wish to save them as dried shelled beans, add another 30 days.

Soil pH: Ideally, 6.0 to 6.5 (slightly acidic).

Beets

A popular root crop, beets are an excellent source of many nutrients, including folic acid and potassium, so why not do something good for yourself and plant a few?

Types: When you think of a beet, you probably think of a round, purplish red root crop, but beets are also found in other colors, including white, orange, and yellow. Try Burpee's Golden for some golden fun! Some varieties are cylindrical, others oval-shaped. Heirloom beets offer lots of variation in shape and color.

Garden Requirements: Shade is tolerated; soil condition is more important than full sun. Aim for a loose, sandy loam for this root crop, not a clay soil. Well-

Beets. *Shutterstock*

rotted manure compost is beneficial. Be careful: Manure that has not composted properly can cause the beets to send off many leaves and shoots, while diminishing the growth of the vegetable itself.

Special Considerations: You can plant these early in the spring; beets are relatively hardy against frost.

Planting Information: Sow your seeds directly into the garden, ½ inch deep, with seeds 1 inch apart, in rows 12 inches apart. Don't expect results overnight or even within a week. Beets are slow to germinate, so don't be surprised if it takes two weeks for your seeds to sprout. Thinning will be necessary later on; beets must be thinned in order to grow properly.

Growing Time: 50 to 60 days for most varieties.

Soil pH: Over 6.0, up to 8.0.

Broccoli

More than one child has been enticed to eat broccoli by enterprising parents who have called the vegetable "trees." If you are fond of these pseudo-trees, give them a try in your garden. You might be pleasantly surprised by how fun they are to grow.

Types: Most broccoli types exhibit the traditional green coloring, but purple is also found. The Green Magic hybrid can be a good choice, or try the Calabrese if you'd like to try an heirloom variety.

Garden Requirements: Broccoli does well in a cool climate with well-drained soil that contains sufficient nitrogen. Sun is good, but partial shade is acceptable, too.

Special Considerations: Seeds can be started indoors. Begin about eight weeks before your last date of frost, then transplant outdoors about five weeks later. You can also purchase seedlings from a garden center.

Planting Information: Sow your broccoli seeds ½ inch deep; sprinkle the seeds and lightly cover. If setting out seedlings, space them 16 to 18 inches apart.

continued

Broccoli. *Shutterstock*

Growing Time: 55 to 65 days. Heirloom varieties may require longer growing time.

Soil pH: 7.0 (neutral).

Brussels sprouts

Brussels sprouts have gotten a bit of a bad rap over the years, but they are actually one of the most interesting vegetables that you can grow. What other vegetable makes such an enchanting spectacle? With their rows of tiny 1- to 2-inch cabbage-like heads along a stalk, Brussels sprouts are a must-have in your garden.

Types: Generally speaking, you have two choices with Brussels sprouts: red or green. Choose the color that best suits your fancy. Long Island Improved is a popular variety that is noted for its high yields.

Garden Requirements: Brussels sprouts enjoy cool weather and can handle a mild frost, but be sure to cover them if you anticipate a hard freeze. Otherwise, plant in full sun, in a sandy loam with good drainage.

Special Considerations: Be aware that Brussels sprouts are unusual in the fact that the plants reach 2 to 4 feet tall and the 1- to 2-inch sprouts grow up along the stem of the plant. Don't be in a rush to harvest your sprouts in autumn; a light autumn frost actually improves the flavor of Brussels sprouts.

Planting Information: Start your seeds indoors, ¼ to ½ inch deep, and then transplant your seedlings outdoors. Place your plants 14 to 24 inches apart, in rows 30 to 36 inches apart.

Growing Time: Brussels sprouts require patience. They need to be started indoors for several weeks, to give you a jumpstart before transplanting outdoors for another 60 to 100 days of outdoor growing.

Soil pH: 7.0 (neutral).

Brussels sprouts.

Cabbage

If you're fond of coleslaw or sauerkraut, be sure to plant at least a few cabbages in your garden. Tight on space? Opt for early varieties that mature quickly and then plant something else in their place.

Types: There are several types of cabbage: early, mid-season, and late. Their sizes are corresponding; early-maturing varieties of cabbage usually weigh about 4 to 6 pounds, while later-maturing varieties can reach up to 16 pounds. Stonehead Hybrid is an early-maturing, green 5-pound cabbage, while Mammoth Red Rock is a 7-pound heirloom variety.

Garden Requirements: Cabbage is best planted in a sunny area of your garden, although some shade is tolerable. Aim for good, fertile soil with lots of nutrients.

Special Considerations: Watch the pH of your soil, and add some lime if your soil is too acidic (under 6.5 pH) for cabbage to be happy.

Planting Information: Start your seeds indoors rather than sowing seed directly into your garden. Plant seeds ¼ to ½ inch deep and 3 inches apart. Later, transplant the seedlings into your garden, planting 18 inches apart for early varieties and 24 inches apart for late varieties. Allow 24 inches between rows.

Growing Time: 58 to 73 days, depending on variety. We've seen super-early varieties that mature in 40 days.

Soil pH: Over 6.5, up to 8.0

Cabbage.

Carrots. *Shutterstock*

Carrots

Carrots are a great source of vitamin A and are also fairly easy to grow. They don't take up much space in the garden, and if grown correctly, carrots are one of the most rewarding vegetables to plant. You can enjoy the tender thinnings as the summer progresses, and then dig in for some hearty carrot treats in the late summer.

Types: From tiny 2-inch Thumbelina carrots all the way up to large 12-inch varieties such as the Envy hybrid, carrots can be found in a wide range of lengths, shapes, and colors, including purple, white, red, yellow, and the traditional orange. For unsurpassed flavor and a fabulous color, try Dragon heirloom carrots!

continued

Garden Requirements: Carrots prefer a cool and wet environment, coupled with a light, sandy soil. The soil must be free of rocks, clay, or manure that hasn't been composted thoroughly.

Special Considerations: About three weeks before your average last date of frost, sow your carrot seed directly into the garden. Mulching will help retain the moisture in the ground. Thinning is almost a necessity.

Planting Information: Carrot seeds are teensy-tiny, and although you'll ideally plant them about ¼ inch deep and about ½ inch apart (in rows about 12 inches apart), it's not always easy to space them exactly as you would like to. Germination takes about two weeks, so be patient.

Growing Time: 58 to 75 days.

Soil pH: Ideally, between 6.5 and 6.8 (slightly acidic), but slightly over or under this range is acceptable.

Cauliflower

Like giant puffy clouds, cauliflower plants are an eye-catching addition to your garden. They also make an impressive addition to a garden box for your county fair. Like most members of the cabbage family, they are fairly easy to grow.

Types: Cauliflower can be found in varying colors, including green, white, or purple heads. The Cheddar Hybrid is a bright orange-yellow color and very impressive.

Garden Requirements: Cool and damp are the main requirements for succeeding with cauliflower. Choose a portion of your garden that receives partial shade, and then work at keeping the ground moist; mulch can be helpful in this respect. Ample water is important for growing cauliflower.

Special Considerations: As a member of the cabbage family, the cauliflower is somewhat hardy and can withstand minor frost. To keep a head white, tie up

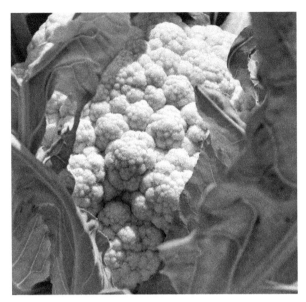

Cauliflower. *Shutterstock*

surrounding leaves to protect it from sunlight as it develops.

Planting Information: As with cabbage and broccoli, start your cauliflower seeds indoors, ¼ to ½ inch deep, 3 inches apart, and then transplant outdoors in rows 18 to 24 inches apart.

Growing Time: This varies widely, from 55 days all the way up to 100 days.

Soil pH: 6.0 to 7.0 (slightly acidic to neutral).

Celery

There are vegetables that are much easier to grow than celery, but if you're up for a bit of a challenge (or if you're a major celery enthusiast), then by all means, go for it.

Types: There's cutting celery, nonblanching celery, and celery for flavoring; there's also celeriac, which is a delectable root that many gardeners enjoy planting. Pascal varieties of celery are very popular; you can get started with Giant Pascal or Summer Pascal.

Garden Requirements: Heavy, moist soil is best for celery plants. You'll need to keep them regularly watered, and it helps if your weather is cool. The ideal soil will have lots of nutrients, as celery "eats" a lot and needs rich soil in order to support itself.

Special Considerations: To achieve success with celery, you need three main components: a long growing season, plenty of cool weather, and plenty of water.

Planting Information: If you can find seedlings, by all means, go ahead and buy them. This will give you a head start in the growing season. But if you can't locate seedlings, you can certainly start your seeds indoors. Plant the seeds about ⅛ inch deep, and keep the planted seeds protected from sunlight. Some gardeners suggest adding a thin layer of moss over the top of the soil until the celery seeds sprout. When you transplant the celery seedlings to your garden, space them between 6 and 12 inches apart, in rows 12 to 18 inches apart.

Growing Time: Celery takes time—and lots of it. Figure on 115 to 135 days to reach maturity.

Soil pH: 6.0 to 7.0 (slightly acidic to neutral).

Celery. *Shutterstock*

Corn. *Shutterstock*

Corn

Corn provides a lot of bang for its buck: You plant a few kernels of corn in the ground, and before long you have tall cornstalks loaded with delicious ears of corn.

Types: Sweet corn is easily the most popular (and delicious!) type of corn for culinary purposes; popcorn is not considered an "eating" corn, except as popcorn; Indian corn has multicolored kernels and is generally used for decorative purposes.

Garden Requirements: In order to thrive, corn needs sunshine. A windbreak is also helpful, as strong winds can blow down your stalks and damage them. Sandy soil will give you the best results.

Special Considerations: Heirloom corn is also known as "open pollinated" corn; in other words, the seeds are savable. Hybrid corn is not open pollinated, but it does produce at a significantly higher rate than heirloom corn.

Planting Information: After last frost, sow in rows, 1 to 2 inches deep, approximately 4 inches apart. Place two seeds per hole, and space your rows 24 inches apart. Plant corn in a block rather than one or two long rows because it is wind pollinated.

continued

Growing Time: 65 to 90 days; some super-early varieties may be ready in less than 55 days. Early maturing hybrids are on the shorter end, open-pollinated varieties are on the longer end.

Soil pH: 6.0 to 7.0 (slightly acidic to neutral). Nitrogen is vital.

Frosty Flavors

Vegetables in the *Brassica oleracea* family are noted for having improved flavor after a light frost. These include broccoli, Brussels sprouts, cabbages, cauliflower, and radishes. This is due to the fact that the frost increases the sugar content in the vegetables, causing a sweeter flavor. Some other vegetables—including leeks, as well as many root vegetables—also have improved flavor after frost, for a similar reason: The starches in these vegetables convert to sugar after frost.

Shutterstock

Cucumbers. *Shutterstock*

Cucumbers

The taste of homegrown cucumbers far exceeds the taste of any cucumber that you can purchase at a grocery store. Fresh, crisp, and light, your garden-fresh cucumbers will undoubtedly delight anyone who has the pleasure of enjoying one.

Types: Pickling and slicing varieties are the two most common types of cucumber. Pickling cucumbers are typically smaller, and slicing cucumbers are larger. You can plant bush varieties and vine varieties; the latter can be trained to climb a trellis, which is helpful for keeping your cucumbers out of the dirt. If you want to try the most delicious cucumber in the entire world (in our opinion), plant True Lemon cucumbers, available from Seed Savers Exchange.

Garden Requirements: Cucumbers love warm weather and lots of sunshine. Well-drained soil is important, as is ample water. If you harvest your cucumbers regularly, you'll keep them producing longer. Also be careful to protect them from frost. Cucumbers do not tolerate frost.

Special Considerations: You can start your cucumbers indoors, but you must be careful not to disturb the roots at transplanting time, as this can stunt the growth of the plants.

Planting Information: Plant your seeds in hills, about 1 inch deep, with approximately 6 seeds per hill. Space your hills in rows approximately 3 feet apart.

Growing Time: You can find early maturing hybrids that can finish out in as little as 45 days, but most cucumbers are in the 50- to 65-day range.

Soil pH: 5.5 to 6.5 (moderately acidic).

Eggplant

Let's be perfectly honest here: Eggplant is fun to grow. If you live in a climate where you can safely grow eggplant, don't delay! Check out the brilliant heirloom varieties that are available from Baker Creek Heirloom Seeds (www.rareseeds.com) or Seed Savers Exchange (www.seedsavers.org).

Types: Many varieties of eggplant are purple, but you can also find varieties in other colors, including green, yellow, and red, as well as eggplant that is literally egg-shaped and white.

Eggplant. *Shutterstock*

Garden Requirements: Eggplant is *very* sensitive to cold weather and should be started indoors if you are in a climate with a short growing season. Plant your seedlings in full sun, in soil with good drainage. Eggplant does not need as much water as some of the other vegetables, but it requires warm temperatures and a rich, sandy soil.

Special Considerations: The weather must be warm.

Planting Information: Start indoors in pots (¼ inch deep), and then transplant into your garden in hills, allowing 2 to 3 feet between hills.

Growing Time: 50 to 80 days, depending on the variety.

Soil pH: Ideally, 6.5, although anything from 5.5 to 7.0 is acceptable.

Garlic

Don't let the bad breath rumors discourage you; garlic is very popular for growing in home gardens and you can grow a lot of garlic from the cloves in one bulb. Be sure to check out the wide selection of heirloom garlic varieties.

Types: Garlic is found in two varieties: hardneck and softneck. Softneck garlic is noted for having a higher number of cloves in comparison to hardneck garlic; softneck garlic also keeps longer than hardneck.

Garden Requirements: Full sun and well-drained soil are the two main requirements for successful garlic growing. In addition to being well drained, your soil should be good quality; loose and sandy is best.

Special Considerations: To plant garlic, purchase garlic bulbs from a catalog or garden center. Each bulb will contain between six and twenty cloves (depending on the variety). You then separate the cloves and plant all but the smallest ones.

Planting Information: Plant your garlic cloves 2 inches apart and approximately 2 inches deep, with the "pointy" end of the clove facing up. Plant directly into the garden. Don't try growing garlic indoors for later transplanting; it isn't a feasible idea.

Growing Time: Growing time is dependent upon whether you plant in the spring or the fall. Generally, it's recommended that you plant in the late autumn and harvest in late spring or early summer.

Soil pH: 5.5 to 6.8 (moderately to slightly acidic).

Garlic. *Shutterstock*

Gourds

You can't eat them (most varieties anyway), but gourds are incredibly fun. With their dizzying array of sizes, shapes, colors, and types, you certainly won't be bored with gourds in your garden.

Gourds. *Shutterstock*

Types: There are many varieties of gourds—as many as you can imagine! Edible gourds are few and far between (look for the Serpente Di Sicila or the Cucuzzi varieties), but decorative gourds (also called craft gourds) are everywhere, and they come in all shapes and sizes. Buy a multivariety seed packet and have fun seeing what comes up.

Garden Requirements: To grow gourds, you need a long growing season. Plant your gourds in full sun, and aim for loose soil. Provide your gourds with regular attention and keep a close eye on them.

Special Considerations: Gourds require climbing assistance in the form of a sturdy trellis or fence.

Planting Information: Start your seeds outdoors in warm climates, or indoors in the north. Sow your seeds ½ inch deep, in hills or rows, generously spaced (over 1 foot).

Growing Time: Gourds require a long growing season: more than 100 days for most varieties. Therefore, consider starting indoors first.

Soil pH: Ideally 6.0 to 6.5 (slightly acidic).

Kale

Kale is exceptionally nutritious—an excellent source of vitamins A and C, in addition to being loaded with calcium and folic acid. With all of those nutritious goodies inside, coupled with the fact that it is a hardy vegetable that can be grown almost anywhere, is there any reason why you wouldn't grow kale in your garden?

Types: There are a few different types of kale: a headless variety, a rutabaga type, and collards. Blue Curled Scotch kale is known for being hardy and easy to grow.

Garden Requirements: Kale is super hardy and will grow virtually anywhere. It likes sun but tolerates the shade and prefers well-drained soil.

Special Considerations: Since kale prefers cooler weather to hot, it's usually best when grown in the spring, early summer, or late autumn. The flavor is better when the temperatures are relatively cool, and imiproves further after light frost.

Planting Information: Sow seeds ½ inch deep, approximately 1 foot apart, in rows 24 to 30 inches apart.

Growing Time: 55 to 70 days.

Soil pH: Over 5.5.

Kale.

Kohlrabi

Why grow kohlrabi? The question should be, why not grow kohlrabi? For one thing, this member of the cabbage family is about as unusual a vegetable as you can grow. It's easy to grow in a variety of climates, and it's fun, too.

Types: Kohlrabi is available in several varieties: white, purple, and king-size. Some say that kohlrabi tastes like turnips; others say it tastes more like apples. Why not grow a few and see for yourself?

Garden Requirements: Kohlrabi prefers good sun and a soil that is well drained. It tolerates cold weather very well.

Special Considerations: Many recommend that you plant kohlrabi in succession, due to the fact that they produce for only a short window of time. If you continue to plant over a period of several weeks, you'll be eating kohlrabi the entire summer.

Planting Information: Kohlrabi can be started indoors or out. It can even be started outdoors weeks before your last date of frost. Sow seeds ¼ to ½ inch deep, with 3 to 6 inches between and 12 inches between rows.

Growing Time: 38 to 62 days. Giant varieties can require upwards of 100 days.

Soil pH: 6.0 to 7.0 (slightly acidic to neutral).

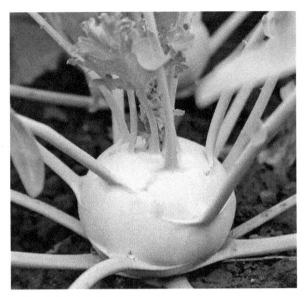

White kohlrabi. *Shutterstock*

Leeks. *Shutterstock*

Leeks

If you have any difficulty in growing traditional bulb onions, then you might want to give leeks a try. Instead of harvesting the bulbs, you instead harvest the stalks, which reach approximately 1 to 2 inches in diameter and provide a similar taste to traditional onions.

Types: Generally speaking, there are two ways to plant leeks: If you live in a Southern climate, you'll probably want to plant them in the fall and harvest them in the spring (called "overwintering leeks"), and if you live in a Northern climate, you'll want to plant them in the spring and harvest them in the autumn (called "summer leeks"). The American Flag variety is very tasty and easy to grow.

Garden Requirements: Leeks love sun, so plant them in a location where they will be sure to benefit from some long days of sunshine.

Special Considerations: Due to the length of time it takes leeks to reach maturity, you'll probably want to start summer leeks indoors 10 to 12 weeks before your desired transplant date.

Planting Information: Start indoors (¼ inch deep), then transplant outdoors, spacing your transplants approximately 3 to 6 inches apart in rows of approximately 24 inches. You can transplant outdoors prior to your last date of frost, as the last bit of cold weather will likely not harm your leeks and will gain you the benefit of some extra growing time.

Growing Time: Over 100, up to 130 days.

Soil pH: 6.0 to 6.8 (slightly acidic).

Lettuce

Everyone needs lettuce in their garden. What would a summer sandwich be without crisp lettuce? Don't get trapped into thinking that your lettuce must be iceberg head lettuce; in fact, you'll probably have better success growing leaf lettuce.

Types: Leaf lettuce varieties are celtuce, looseleaf, and romaine; head lettuce varieties are butterhead and crisphead. (Crisphead, also known as iceberg, is the type that you see in the grocery store: the big head of pale green lettuce with thick, tasteless leaves.) Black Seeded Simpson leaf lettuce is a tried-and-true variety (pick it early, as it becomes slightly bitter if left too long). We also love Forellenschuss; unfortunately, so do the squirrels!

Garden Requirements: Lettuce doesn't need (or want!) good sun; instead, find a shady place. You can nestle your lettuce plants between other plants to save space and to give them some shade. Loose soil with plenty of nitrogen is best.

Lettuce.

Special Considerations: Heat ruins lettuce by causing it to bolt (go to seed). Iceberg lettuce is particularly prone to bolting. Many gardeners find that it is much easier to grow looseleaf lettuce, as it is much less prone to bolting.

Planting Information: Plant early, prior to the last date of frost, and again in late summer for a fall crop. Sow ½ inch deep, ½ inch apart, unless planting leaf lettuce, which can be sown in a continuous row (although it will have to be thinned later).

Growing Time: Leaf lettuce: 40 to 45 days. Head lettuce: 80 to 95 days.

Soil pH: 6.0 to 7.0 (slightly acidic to neutral).

Okra

If you love gumbo, you might want to try growing okra.

Types: The most common variety of okra is the Clemson Spineless variety, although there are other hybrid and heirloom varieties available.

Garden Requirements: Okra needs warmth; cold weather inhibits growth, so be sure to wait until the soil is sufficiently warm (over 65 degrees Fahrenheit at
continued

Okra. *Shutterstock*

Planting Information: Sow seeds ¾ to 1 inch deep, directly into your garden. Leave 6 to 18 inches between your seeds or plants, and space your rows 1 to 3 feet apart. If you must start your okra seeds early indoors, then you'll want to plant them in larger pots so that you will not disturb the seedlings upon transplant. In either case, soaking the seeds overnight before planting is recommended.

Growing Time: 50 to 60 days.

Soil pH: 6.0 to 7.0 (slightly acidic to neutral).

Onions

Permit us a moment of personal opinion: We love growing bulb onions. They are some of the most satisfying vegetables we've ever grown. There is something almost magical about the way they grow, and it's simply fun to harvest them.

Types: Long-day or short-day—what's the difference? Contrary to what you might think, long-day onions are the type that you'll want to grow if you live in a northern climate, and short-day onions are the type that you'll want to grow if you live in a southern climate. There are also day-neutral varieties, such as the Candy Hybrid (our favorite!) that are suitable for growing in a wide range of locations. You can find red, yellow, or white onions in both long- and short-day varieties, so just shop around until you find the combination that you're looking for.

Garden Requirements: Sandy soil or a sandy loam is best for growing onions. Top this off with ample sunshine and regular watering (mulching with grass clippings helps keep the soil moist) and you'll be well on your way to growing some marvelous onions.

Special Considerations: For those with short growing seasons, start with onion sets or plants rather than seed. Onion sets are tiny bulbs that you can purchase at garden centers or in seed catalogs, while onion plants are already growing and can save you even more time.

a depth of 4 inches) before you attempt planting. The ideal soil is a good loam with nice drainage.

Special Considerations: Okra grows rapidly and becomes very tall (heights of 2 to 9 feet), so the plants may end up shading your other plants if you're not careful about placement. Consider this when you select the location for your okra plants in your garden. Also, be careful and use gloves when handling okra plants; the stems can be rather prickly and can cause irritation to your hands and arms.

Onions.

Planting Information: If planting from sets or plants, space the individual plants 2 to 4 inches apart, in rows 12 to 18 inches apart. Onions tolerate cold, so you can plant these sets before your last date of frost. If you wish to start from seed, then you'll want to start them indoors a few weeks earlier.

Growing Time: There's a wide variance: 85 to 160 days, depending on the variety.

Soil pH: Above 6.0 up to about 7.0 (slightly acidic to neutral). Supplement with lime if necessary.

Parsnips

If you like growing carrots and are up to a bit of a challenge, you're likely to enjoy the opportunity to grow parsnips as well.

Types: Most varieties of parsnip resemble a white or cream-colored carrot. Popular varieties include Harris Model and All America, both of which are white.

Garden Requirements: As they are very similar to carrots, parsnips enjoy similar soil, a midrange loam without too much sand or clay. Parsnips don't require quite as much water as some of the other vegetables, but the soil should be kept slightly damp.

Special Considerations: Be sure to work your ground well before planting to ensure that your parsnips have a place to grow. They are root plants that will reach underground lengths of up to 12 inches, so allow plenty of loosened space for them to achieve their full length. Exposure to cold improves the flavor, so harvest your parsnips in late fall after a few frosts. If your climate allows it, you can continue to harvest them throughout the winter, especially if you add at least 6 inches of straw on top of your parsnip bed. A final option is to leave parsnips in the ground during winter and harvest them in the early spring.

Planting Information: Sow your seeds ¼ inch deep—no more than that. Aim for ½ inch apart, and space your rows 24 inches apart. And then wait—and wait. The germination time for parsnips is slower than many other vegetables.

Growing Time: Parsnips are slowpokes. They're slow to germinate, slow to grow, slow, slow, slow—a minimum of 110 to 130 days. Allow the entire summer and into the fall before you begin harvesting. If you're especially patient, you can wait until the next spring to harvest.

Soil pH: 5.5 to 7.0 (moderately acidic to neutral).

Parsnips. *Shutterstock*

Peas. *Shutterstock*

Peas

Who doesn't love peas? If you don't, perhaps it's because you haven't encountered the delight of fresh, homegrown peas. They're so good you won't want to hide them under your plate anymore!

Types: There are many different types of peas to choose from—dwarf varieties that are bushlike, as well taller varieties that require support. Green Arrow peas, for instance, only need minimal support, as the plants do not grow beyond approximately 24 inches. If you want to plant peas with edible pods, look for "sugar" or "snow" peas. English (also known as "garden" or "shell") peas must have the pods removed before you eat them. We have enjoyed planting Golden Sweet heirloom peas; for the best flavor, they should be harvested before the pods reach full maturity.

Garden Requirements: You can plant your peas very early in the spring; sow them outdoors six to eight weeks before the last date of frost. Peas enjoy cool weather and plenty of water. Your early-spring crops should be planted in full sun, but if you try for crops in the summer, you might want to plant them in a location with a bit of shade.

Special Considerations: Dwarf varieties may not need support, but most varieties will require the presence of a trellis or fence.

Planting Information: Sow your seeds directly into the garden (no need to start them indoors first), approximately 1 inch deep. Space your seeds about 2 to 3 inches apart, in rows about 12 to 18 inches apart.

Growing Time: 56 to 73 days.

Soil pH: The entire range of 6.0 to 8.0 is acceptable, but 6.0 to 6.5 (slightly acidic) is best.

Peppers

The pepper is another one of those vegetables that is vastly better when homegrown. A freshly picked sweet bell pepper, straight out of the garden, is one of the choicest treats we can imagine. Sweet peppers are handy because they begin maturing at about the same time as tomatoes and cucumbers, and the three of them make beautiful salads together. Hot peppers are not for the faint of heart, but they are exciting to grow if simply for the amazing colors and shapes they produce.

Types: The two main pepper classifications are hot and sweet. Both come in a range of shapes and a rainbow of colors: green, red, yellow, purple, and many more. Some

Sweet peppers. *Shutterstock*

popular hot peppers include jalapeños, poblanos, and habaneros (the hottest). Look for heirloom pepper varieties such as Fish (hot) and Purple Beauty (sweet) to add a bit of excitement to your garden.

Garden Requirements: Lots of sunshine is important for the success of your pepper plants. A good-quality soil, light and loamy, is suitable for peppers. They thrive on warmth and do not like frost. Keep them indoors until you're positive that the temperatures are sufficiently warm in the spring and there's no danger of a late-spring frost, and be ready to cover or pick your produce in the autumn if an early frost is imminent.

Special Considerations: Hot peppers are exactly as their name implies: hot. As you probably know, they are hot to eat, but they can also wreak havoc on your hands if you're not careful. Exercise caution when handling your peppers and wear rubber gloves to protect yourself.

Planting Information: The fact that peppers need an ample growing season, coupled with the fact that they are very frost-sensitive, means that you'll need to extend your growing season in some fashion. Starting indoors is the best way to achieve this. Start the seeds in flats at a depth of ⅛ to ¼ inch deep. When the seedlings are about 2 inches tall, you can transplant them to larger containers, and by the time they are about 6 inches tall (approximately six to ten weeks after starting the seeds), you'll be ready to put them outdoors. Space them approximately 12 to 18 inches apart in the garden, allowing about 2 feet between rows. Peppers don't spread out the way tomatoes do, so it's easier to grow more plants in a smaller space.

Growing Time: 65 to 80 days.

Soil pH: 5.5 to 6.8 (moderately to slightly acidic).

Potatoes

Potatoes are the underground treasure of the garden. They're packed with nutrients, and they're said to

Potatoes.

produce one of the highest yields per acre of any food crop.

Types: There's a potato to suit everyone's fancy—whether you'd like a quicker maturing or slower maturing variety; or whether you'd like white, yellow, blue, red, or a host of other potato colors. Some varieties are noted for being excellent baking potatoes (Yukon Gold, for instance), while other varieties are exceptionally good for mashing, such as the Red Pontiac.

Garden Requirements: As you'll remember, root vegetables such as carrots and parsnips like a light, loamy soil that isn't too heavy. The same is true of potatoes. Avoid planting your potatoes in the same location year after year; it's better to move them around to new locations.

Special Considerations: Harvesting potatoes is fun, since you get to dig up these delightful starchy treasures from underground. If you wish to harvest "new potatoes," you can do so as soon as they have reached a sufficient size for eating. A new potato is not completely mature and not suitable for storage, but if you plan to eat them immediately, they are a treat. For the rest of your potatoes, you'll want to wait until

continued

they are fully mature before digging them up. Watch the plant leaves; when they are turning yellow and brown in the autumn, it's probably time to harvest the potatoes. It's common, but not necessary, to wait until after the first frost to harvest potatoes. Potato stalks and leaves are poisonous, as are the "sprouts" that grow out of the potato and any green spots on the potato. Do not consume any of those.

Planting Information: You don't have to wait around for the weather to warm up before you begin planting potatoes. To prepare your seed potatoes for planting, allow them to sit in a sunny area for a few days so that they begin sprouting. Then chop them up into smaller chunks, making sure that each chunk contains at least one "eye," or sprout. Leave them for a couple of days, and then plant your potato "chunks" by placing them in a furrow about 4 to 6 inches deep, about 6 inches apart. Position the chunks with the eye toward the sky, then fill in the trench with a couple of inches of soil. As the potato plant begins to grow and is visible above the ground, keep adding additional soil in a hill-like manner around the plant.

Growing Time: 80 to 120 days, depending on the variety.

Soil pH: 5.0 to 6.0 (acidic). Not over 6.0.

Pumpkins

Pumpkins are a happy vegetable to grow. There's something magical about the feelings that a pumpkin evokes—special, happy, holiday feelings. In addition to this, pumpkins are simply fun to grow. They're fun to pick, they're fun to carve, and they're fun to eat. Are you convinced yet?

Types: Don't be fooled into thinking that all pumpkins are orange. Not only are pumpkins found in a wealth of additional colors (white and blue, for instance), they also come in a huge range of sizes, from palm-size all the way up to a record-setting 1,600-pound

Pumpkins. *Shutterstock*

giant. If you're looking for something substantial, try Big Max, which matures to over 100 pounds. Or if petite suits your fancy, look for Jack-Be-Little. Other options include the mid-size Connecticut Field or the blue Jarrahdale, both heirlooms. Don't be fooled into thinking that all pumpkins are round, either. The Rouge vif d'Etampes, also known as the Cinderella pumpkin, is flatter with deep ridges along the sides. Have fun selecting the type of pumpkin that suits your fancy.

Garden Requirements: Full sun and well-drained soil. These are important, as is the presence of lots of well-composted manure. The nitrogen in the manure helps facilitate the growth of top-quality pumpkins. You'll also need plenty of space—although bush varieties such as Bushkin require less space than vine varieties such as Connecticut Field. Bush varieties are also quicker to mature, but vine varieties are generally more popular.

Special Considerations: Growing pumpkins is much the same as growing winter squash, which makes sense, since that's exactly what a pumpkin is. So you'll need a long growing season, plenty of space, and good soil. If you decide to transplant, be very careful—pumpkin plants don't handle transplanting very well.

Planting Information: You can start pumpkin seeds indoors, or you can sow them directly into the garden. Your objective is to get them going as soon as possible, with the caveat that the weather must be warm (the soil temperature should reach at least 65 degrees Fahrenheit at a depth of 4 inches) before the seeds (or seedlings) are set out. If sowing outdoors, plant 1 inch deep in hills, with 4 to 6 seeds per hill, with plenty of space (3 to 6 feet) between the hills. Your pumpkins will want plenty of space to spread out and take over, although bush varieties require slightly less space than vine varieties.

Growing Time: 90 to 140 days; most varieties average in the 100- to 120-day range.

Soil pH: 5.5 to 7.5 (very adaptable).

Radishes.

Radishes

Radishes are one of the earliest spring crops. They can be planted early, and their rapid germination and rapid growth mean that you could be enjoying radishes long before anything else in your garden.

Types: You can find red, white, or yellow radishes, but the most common type is the red "cherry"-shaped radish. Try the Early Scarlet Belle variety if you're in a hurry (23 days) or Snow Belle if you don't mind waiting a bit longer (30 days); the latter is a snowy white color.

Garden Requirements: A loose, sandy soil will do nicely; radishes don't require a lot of nitrogen, but they do appreciate full sun.

Special Considerations: If you're also planting carrots, consider planting your radishes with them. The quick germination of radishes helps gardeners easily locate the planting location of the slower germinating carrots.

Planting Information: Sow your radishes directly into your garden; there's no need to start them indoors first. Plant your radishes ¼ to ½ inch deep, spaced about 2 inches apart. The rows don't need to be very far apart; radishes are tiny, so you only need to allow a few inches between the rows.

Growing Time: Quick! As little as 20 days, although some varieties require up to 60 days.

Soil pH: 5.8 to 6.8 (moderately to slightly acidic).

Building a Sunflower House

"All work and no play makes Jack a dull boy," as the old saying goes. And the perfect way to combine play with vegetable gardening is to build a sunflower house.

Designate a space in your garden (6 × 6 feet, 8 × 8 feet, or whatever works for you) and plant the perimeter with sunflower seeds (be sure to leave an opening for a "door"). Choose a tall variety of sunflower so that your house will be large enough for children to play inside, but be careful not to plant them where they will shade your vegetables. When the sunflowers have reached a height of over 6 feet, you can create a "roof" by fastening the tops of the sunflower together with string, thereby enclosing the house. If you plant your house in a grassy area (making a 1-foot garden bed around the perimeter just large enough to plant your sunflowers), then your house will have a soft, green carpet inside—how nice!

Rhubarb

Rhubarb is a perennial and will return year after year, so site selection is important. You can plant rhubarb in the same bed as your asparagus, and the two plants can perennialize together!

Types: Most rhubarb types have green stalks. However, you can find varieties with red stalks; try Crimson Red.

Garden Requirements: Full sun is ideal, but some shade is tolerated. Good drainage cannot be overemphasized; it's very important to the success of your rhubarb. Because it is a perennial, deep cultivation of the soil is also essential. As is the case with asparagus, you won't have the opportunity in years to come to replenish the soil with manure, so consider this in advance.

Special Considerations: Rhubarb has long been obtained by sharing between neighbors; it transplants very well by division. If you have a neighbor, friend, or relative with rhubarb plants, they would probably be more than willing to give you a portion of their own abundant supply with which to start your own plant. If not, you can purchase rhubarb roots from a nursery. **The leaves of rhubarb are poisonous; don't eat them.**

Planting Information: To plant your rhubarb roots, dig a deep hole or trench (2 feet deep is typical), then fill most of it with well-composted manure. Make a mound of soil in the hole or trench, and set the rhubarb roots on top. Then fill in with soil, burying the crown of the roots by about 2 inches.

Growing Time: Rhubarb is hardy in Zones 3 to 8, but you can grow it even in Zone 2 with a little extra effort. As is the case with asparagus, you won't harvest any rhubarb the first season, and only minimally the second.

Soil pH: 5.5 to 6.5 (moderately acidic).

Rhubarb. *Shutterstock*

Spinach

Popeye notwithstanding, there are many reasons to grow spinach. For one thing, it's simply loaded with nutrition. For another, it's one of the best early-season crops, so you can get started with spinach while you're waiting to plant some of your other vegetables.

Spinach.

continued

Types: Savoy, semi-savoy, and flat-leaf are the spinach varieties. Savoy spinach has curly leaves; flat-leaf has (you guessed it!) flat leaves. Try Bloomsdale Long Standing for a savoy variety or Giant Noble if you prefer flat-leaf spinach.

Garden Requirements: Spinach prefers a light, loamy soil with lots of nutrients. It also likes cool weather rather than hot. You can plant in sun or partial shade; either is suitable.

Special Considerations: Spinach likes to bolt (go to seed), and when it bolts, it ceases to grow new leaves. Spinach is particularly prone to bolting if the weather gets warm, so plant early in the spring or in late summer/early autumn when the days are shorter and the temperatures cooler.

Planting Information: Go ahead and get started early in the spring. Sow your seeds directly into the garden. It's not necessary to start them indoors, because you can sow them outdoors a couple of weeks before the average last date of frost. Plant ¼ to ½ inch deep, allowing 6 to 12 inches between plants and 12 to 18 inches between rows.

Growing Time: 40 to 65 days.

Soil pH: 6.0 to 7.0 (slightly acidic to neutral).

Squash (Summer)

We love growing summer squash. All right, in all honesty, we love growing winter squash, too—but summer squash is incredibly fun for its abundant production.

Types: There are many types of summer squash, including zucchini, yellow straight-neck, yellow crookneck, scallop (also known as patty-pan, a small round squash with scalloped edges), and many others.

Garden Requirements: Sun and good drainage are vital for the success of your summer squash. It requires a nutritious soil, and warmth is essential.

Summer squash.

Special Considerations: Summer squash requires ample space in your garden, but it makes up for the space by providing ample production in return.

Planting Information: You can start your summer squash seeds indoors or out; we've had equal success with both methods, but their short growing season makes them a good candidate for planting directly into your garden. If you do start them indoors, be very careful when transplanting; their root systems are very sensitive. Indoors or out, plant your seeds 1 inch deep; if outdoors, plant in hills, with four to six seeds per hill (you'll thin them later).

Growing Time: Summer squash is quick to pop out the produce; figure on 42 to 50 days for most varieties. Don't assume that larger is necessarily better; many types of summer squash are best to eat when 6 to 8 inches long, although scallop squash are harvested when they are about 2 to 3 inches in diameter.

Soil pH: 6.0 to 7.5.

Squash (Winter)

Winter squash takes patience to grow—lots of patience. Since patience has never been Samantha's greatest virtue, we have better success with summer squash. If you are endowed with more patience, you could have a lot of fun growing winter squash.

Types: Acorn, hubbard, butternut, spaghetti, buttercup, also pumpkin (see separate entry).

Garden Requirements: You need lots of space to grow winter squash. They like nothing better than to spread out and take over your garden, so beware. In addition to ample space, you want a sunny location and a nutrient-rich soil.

Special Considerations: Don't be in any hurry to harvest your winter squash. Summer squash and winter squash are entirely different things—and winter squash needs plenty of time to fully mature.

Planting Information: You'll want to start winter squash seeds indoors, but be very careful when transplanting so that you don't disturb the roots. Plant 1 inch deep, in hills, and transplant with about 4 to 6 feet between seedlings.

Growing Time: Some hybrids have been developed for earliness, but you would be hard-pressed to find any that grow in less than 70 days, and that's a little acorn squash. Figure on at least 90 and up to 140 days for most winter squash plants.

Soil pH: 5.5 to 7.0 (moderately acidic to neutral).

Tomatoes

Tomatoes are super-easy to grow and provide a great return on your efforts. You can choose from an impressive rainbow of varieties, in all shapes, sizes, and colors, and at harvest time you can use them in a wide range of dishes. We love tomatoes, and grow at least fifteen varieties each year!

Types: Tomatoes are found in two main types: determinate and indeterminate. The differences are simple: Determinate varieties are shorter, more

Winter squash. *Shutterstock*

Cherry tomatoes.

continued

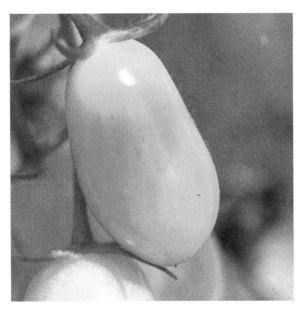
Yellow tomatoes.

mosaic virus is indicated by T. Heirloom varieties, while not exhibiting the resistance that the newer varieties boast, do have an advantage in the fact that you can save their seeds. Additionally, there are the flavor benefits, which are marvelous indeed. Many people select the Brandywine variety for its flavor, while others prefer Cherokee Purple. Our favorite heirlooms are the Wapsipinicon Peach and the Green Zebra. Our favorite hybrid is Juliet; it is prolific, tasty, and resistant to cracking.

Garden Requirements: Sunshine and plenty of regular watering.

Special Considerations: For indeterminate varieties, you'll need tomato cages to hold up their sprawling and flourishing branches. Some people allow their indeterminate tomatoes to grow on the ground in a vinelike appearance, but you'll harvest higher yields if you use tomato cages, in addition to the fact that they keep your tomatoes off the ground, which results in cleaner tomatoes and keeps them out of the mouths of small rodents.

Many gardeners say that you need only six tomato plants to provide you with all the produce you need, but we never plant fewer than thirty seedlings and we've never had any trouble using up the hundreds of tomatoes that they produce.

Planting Information: You can start your seeds indoors, or you can buy seedlings. Typically, it's tough to start seeds outdoors. Tomatoes want warm soil, so seedlings are the way to go. For seeds, start in flats or peat pots, planting the seeds about ¼ inch deep (go ½ inch if you sow directly outdoors). When the seedlings reach 2 to 3 inches tall, transplant to larger containers if you started them in flats; otherwise, wait until they reach about 6 inches before transplanting outdoors (assuming, of course, that the weather is satisfactory).

It's wise to plant tomatoes using the "trenching" method, which doesn't necessarily have to involve a trench. Basically, it means that you plant the seedlings with a good portion of their stem underground. Some people plant them literally sideways, then curve the

"bushy" plants that produce for a limited period of time (i.e., the growing time is precisely determined). Determinates are ideal for small gardens where space is at a premium or for growing in containers. Indeterminate varieties grow and spread throughout the season and produce continually (i.e., the growing time is not precisely determined). They produce a higher volume of tomatoes but require much more space.

Within both types, there are myriad colors and shapes. You can find cherry tomatoes, romas, egg-shaped, and the traditional round tomatoes. As far as colors, the rainbow is virtually limitless: green, white, yellow, purple, pink, red, orange, and even striped.

Another thing to remember: Tomatoes are found in heirloom and hybrid varieties. Many of the hybrids have been carefully developed for resistance to diseases and pests. You'll see letters after the names of hybrids, such as Better Boy (VFN), which means it is resistant to verticillium wilt disease (V), fusarium wilt race 1 (F), and root-knot nematodes (N). If a variety is also resistant to fusarium wilt race 2, the designation is FF, and a resistance to tobacco stem upward so that the top portion is above ground. This type of planting system allows your tomato seedlings to establish a strong foundation of roots, as new roots will grow underground all along the stem.

Growing Time: 70 to 85 days. Some hybrid varieties are known for their short growing times; for example, the Early Girl matures in 52 days.

Soil pH: 6.0 to 6.8 (slightly acidic).

Heirloom tomatoes. *Shutterstock*

Hybrid tomatoes.

Chapter 6

Veggie Sidekicks: Herbs and Fruits

If you'd like to expand your food garden beyond vegetables, consider growing a few herbs and fruits. They make wonderful additions to any garden. In this chapter, we'll give you some basic information on several culinary herbs as well as popular fruits that are easy to grow.

Herbs

Herbs are relatively easy to grow and thrive in a variety of situations. They add a touch of beauty and elegance to your garden, especially if you intersperse them among your vegetable plants. Their delicate foliage and sweet fragrances are almost flower-like.

Most county fairs provide categories for exhibiting herbs, although the requirements for presentation do vary from one fair to another. Some ask that the cut herbs be exhibited with a tiny plastic bag on the end; others ask that you display the cut herbs in tiny glass containers, while others allow you to place the herbs directly on a paper plate. Always follow all rules of your particular fair.

As with vegetable exhibitions, you want your herbs to be fresh, fresh, fresh. Select fully mature examples with good color and fragrance.

The fun thing about growing herbs is that there's absolutely no limit to where you can grow them—in the country, in the city, indoors, or outdoors. Most types are perfectly content to grow indoors in a container nestled in a sunny window.

When you go to purchase your herbs, you may notice that several are only hardy in Zones 5 to 9. If you live in a cooler zone, they will grow as annuals, not perennials.

Basil

You'll be impressed by the rich, dark green leaves of basil—unless, of course, you've planted purple-leaved basil! Basil enjoys full sun and does not flourish in cool weather. For these reasons, basil makes an excellent choice for container-growing indoors. Allow 85 to 90 days to mature.

> **TIP**
>
> The fun thing about growing herbs is that there's absolutely no limit to where you can grow them—in the country, in the city, indoors, or outdoors. Most types are perfectly content to grow indoors in a container nestled in a sunny window.

Basil.

Chives

If you want a sure chance of success, then rush out and plant some chives. These spartans of the onion family survive and thrive when conditions are seemingly against them. Chives are perennial, and they're the first thing we see popping up through the last bits of snow in the early spring. They grow, they spread, and they pop up in new places. This can be kind of fun, but you do have to watch out, or else your chives will promptly take over your entire garden bed. On the other hand, they are pretty, they're fragrant, and they're delicious when added to potato salads or other summer delicacies.

To plant, you can start from seed, or you can divide a portion from a friend who has a chive plant. Either way, chives are easy to grow and win the award for determination.

Bee Balm

We think that everyone should grow bee balm. The name alone conjures up soothing visions of peacefully buzzing bees, and bee balm does in fact attract these helpful garden aids. Brushing your hands on the flowers produces an amazing aromatic scent, and it is a popular herb for use in teas. You may find that this perennial grows too large for container gardening; bee balm can achieve a height of 4 feet.

Chives.

Bee balm.

Lavender

"Lavender's blue, dilly dilly, lavender's green," are the lyrics of the old song, but lavender is actually more of a purple. There are also pink and white varieties. Lavender is occasionally used in cooking, but it also has a multitude of uses ranging from medicinal to cosmetic; it's also a favorite for potpourris and sachets. Plant plenty; it's pretty.

Lavender. *Shutterstock*

Oregano

Oregano is the herb to plant if you're fond of Italian cuisine. Grow oregano indoors or out—just look for a sunny location with good drainage. Oregano reaches a height of 12 to 24 inches when mature and is as lovely to look at as it is tasty to eat.

Oregano. *Shutterstock*

Parsley

A sprig of parsley on the edge of your plate—what a nice touch to enliven your home cooking! Grow in containers or outdoors, selecting a site with good access to sunshine and good soil. Parsley is a biennial, which means that it ought to come up again the second spring after planting. There are a few different varieties of parsley: the commonly found Italian parsley, frilly-edged curly-leaf parsley, and flat-leaf Hamburg parsley.

Parsley. *Shutterstock*

Peppermint

Everyone needs to grow some peppermint in their garden. It's fragrant, it's pretty, and it grows and grows and grows. Be careful, though—it will spread its way through your garden if you don't keep it contained. Peppermint plants can reach up to 3 feet tall, and can be planted in a partially shady location, if necessary.

Peppermint. *Shutterstock*

Rosemary

In addition to being a pretty name for a girl, rosemary is a tasty herb that is added to many delectable dishes, including cakes, casseroles, and meats, especially lamb. Rosemary does very well as a potted plant; it does not thrive in cold weather and prefers warmth, so consider this when planting. Rosemary is an attractive plant with the appearance of pine needles and delightful blue flowers. It's an annual in cool climates and perennial in warm areas with mild winters.

Sage.

Rosemary.

Tarragon

A popular herb for seasoning chicken, tarragon is a valuable herb to plant even if you're not a poultry aficionado. It's also excellent for use in salad dressings. The two main types are French tarragon and Russian tarragon, with the former enjoying more popularity. Tarragon does best in full sun with sandy soil.

Sage

Remember Laura Ingalls arguing with her sister Mary in the classic *Little House on the Prairie* series? Laura wanted sage in the turkey stuffing and Mary did not. Neither won—they ended up not having a turkey.

Sage is a popular seasoning for stuffing, and the plant's beautifully textured leaves are as lovely as they are tasty. There are reportedly nine hundred species of sage in existence; some of the most common include golden sage, purple sage, pineapple sage, and broad-leaf sage.

Tarragon. *Shutterstock*

Thyme

It's time for you to plant some thyme! There's common thyme, lemon thyme, and dwarf thyme—definitely a type for every gardener's needs. Thyme likes sunshine and isn't picky about soil quality; it thrives well in a container. Most thyme varieties mature to about 12 inches tall and produce huge numbers of tiny pastel flowers, which are edible.

Thyme. *Shutterstock*

Fruits

If you'd like to expand your garden beyond vegetables, then consider adding a few fruits to your garden. We'll give you some basic information on apples, pears, berries, and grapes—fun fruits for anyone to enjoy!

Apples

Apples are not a crop that provides instant gratification. You need patience and perseverance for success. Apple trees, on average, will not bear fruit for several years after planting—but don't let this deter you from getting started. Remember the old saying, "The best time to plant a tree is twenty years ago."

Apples.

In order to grow apples, you need to plant at least two apple trees of different varieties. This is because apple trees require cross-pollination in order to bear fruit. Bees will transfer the pollen from one tree to the other.

All apple trees are not created equal; they come in several different sizes. Standard trees are the traditional-size trees, like those you may have seen in old orchards and on farms. Standard trees achieve an average height of 25 to 30 feet. Dwarf trees are just what their name implies: smaller versions of larger trees. Dwarf trees mature to about 10 feet tall and bear fewer apples overall; their fruit, however, grows to the same size as the fruit on standard trees. Semi-dwarf trees are the middle-of-the-road version, taller than a dwarf tree but shorter than a standard tree. Semi-dwarfs mature to approximately 15 to 22 feet. If space is an issue—and for many gardeners it is—you may opt to plant dwarf trees.

Apple trees need well-drained soil and plenty of sunshine in order to thrive. Many apple varieties do best in Zones 4 through 8, but there are several cold-hardy varieties that do well in Zone 3.

Blueberries

Blueberries are a fruit crop in which success has thus far eluded us. Our harsh Wisconsin winters and cool summers undoubtedly play a part, and it's possible our soil isn't acidic enough. Don't let our trials deter you from trying to grow blueberries yourself. They are delectable, delightful, and delicious!

Blueberries thrive best in acidic soil, definitely less than 6.0 pH and ideally more like 4.5 to 5.0. Regular watering is another important consideration—and full sun is always a plus.

There are three main varieties of blueberry: highbush, half-high, and lowbush. Their individual sizes align with their names, thus for container gardening, choose lowbush varieties. For larger, more impressive plants, select highbush varieties.

To plant blueberries, you'll buy established plants; most range between 12 and 18 inches in height, but you'll still have to wait a couple of years before you can anticipate any type of harvest. Some garden centers now offer larger, more mature blueberry plants (at a higher price, of course!), giving you the advantage of buying older plants that will produce much faster.

Grapes

Grapes are undeniably rewarding if you are successful in getting them to produce for you.

Blueberries. *Shutterstock*

Grapes.

Tree Guards

Your young fruit trees are at risk of having their trunks attacked by small animals, so you might wish to purchase tree guards. Available at any nursery or through garden supply catalogs, these plastic trunk protectors keep your tree trunks safe from harm. Tree guards are a relatively inexpensive item that can help protect your tree investment.

Grapes grow on vines and require the presence of something on which to climb. A fence works well for this, as does a stone wall or a trellis. Grapes need plenty of sunshine and warm temperatures in order to thrive—so plant them in full sun. Pruning is an important part of grape growing, and it requires a lot of knowledge in order to do it correctly.

Pears

As is the case with apple trees, pear trees can be purchased in dwarf, semi-dwarf, and standard sizes. Pears are not quite as tolerant to cold weather as apple trees; most varieties are only hardy in Zones 5 to 8. Cold-tolerant varieties can be found, however, so don't give up hope if you live in Zone 4 and have your heart set on a pear tree. Just do a little investigative work to locate varieties that are suitable for your area.

Again, as with apples, plant your pear trees in full sun. Don't be surprised if it takes a few years for your pear tree to bear fruit—it's worth the wait.

Raspberries and Blackberries

We list these together because they are very similar in looks, taste, growth habits, and garden requirements.

Raspberries and blackberries do best in full sun, although we've had success with partial shade as well. Rich, loamy soil with excellent drainage is important. To reduce the incidence of verticillium wilt, do not plant your berry bushes where you have grown tomatoes, potatoes, eggplant, or peppers.

Blackberries benefit from the establishment of some type of sturdy trellis system.

Be careful! Raspberry canes are only slightly scratchy, but certain varieties of blackberries produce canes that are *very* thorny and can be quite painful. Avoid the thorns by wearing long sleeves and gloves whenever you are working with your bushes. Or you can bypass the problem completely by planting thornless varieties.

Pears.

Raspberries. *Shutterstock*

Blackberries. *Shutterstock*

TIP

Raspberries and blackberries benefit from the establishment of some type of sturdy trellis system.

Strawberries

There are two main types of strawberries: June-bearing and everbearing. The former produces berries for only a short period of time (June, incidentally), setting all of its fruit more or less at once. Everbearing strawberries continue producing all season.

Strawberries are relatively hardy and aren't terribly fussy with regard to their growing conditions. Actually, the most difficulty we've encountered with growing strawberries has come in the form of ground squirrels helping themselves to our choicest specimens.

You can start with strawberry plants for the quickest results. Space them in neat little rows, or you can arrange them in a garden bed, making sure to leave about 12 inches between each plant. Strawberries like to send out "runners" (which subsequently become new plants), and this can kind of eliminate the purpose of your rows in the first place.

Strawberries like sunshine and well-drained, fertile soil. Regular weeding is important to achieve best results with your strawberries.

Watermelon

We can't say enough good things about growing watermelon. It's one of the most entertaining things you can plant. Although technically a fruit, it has plenty in common with vegetables—namely that it is an annual you need to plant every year.

Watermelons come in the large, traditional size you see in the grocery store as well as smaller sizes called icebox or lunchbox. Most varieties require 90 to 100 days to mature; Baker Creek Heirloom Seeds (www.rareseeds. com) offers a couple of heirloom varieties that mature in 70 days—good for northern climates.

The best soil is a light loam, not heavy, well tilled with lots of nutrients, and slightly acidic (5.5 to 6.8 pH). Fusarium wilt and powdery mildew can strike

Strawberries. *Shutterstock*

watermelon. Crop rotation is important in order to minimize your incidences of these diseases.

The plants like sun, sun, sun! Watermelon does not tolerate cold weather. Wait until after the danger of frost has passed before sowing seeds outdoors (1 inch deep, 4 to 12 feet apart). It has a sensitive root system, making transplanting difficult. If you do opt to start indoors, try using peat pots to avoid root disturbance and transplant the entire pot to the garden (when seedlings are 3 to 4 inches tall).

Watermelon. *Shutterstock*

Chapter 7

Exhibiting Your Produce

Your goals for your garden may be two- or threefold. You may wish to grow food for your own consumption. You might also desire to grow vegetables for exhibition at a county fair or state fair, or perhaps you want to grow surplus produce to sell at farmers' markets or via other venues. For the purposes of this chapter, we'll focus on preparing vegetable garden exhibits for the fair.

Planning Ahead

Your first step is to find out the date of your fair. Let's say it's the first week of August. You want your produce to be at its peak at that time. If you wanted to exhibit peas at the county fair and didn't plan ahead, then your first pea crop that you planted back in early May would have long since passed by the time August 1 rolled around. Make a note on your calendar to sow an extra planting of 55-day peas around June 1.

Similarly, if your wish is to exhibit prize-winning pumpkins at the fair, you may find yourself scratching your head. How will you have fully grown and mature pumpkins ready to exhibit in early August? Pumpkins, as you may recall, require a growing time of 90 to 130 days, and if you've just planted seeds in late May, you may be in trouble. To avoid this situation, you'll need to think ahead. Start your seeds early—indoors—to give your plants an added boost of several growing weeks early in the season. In order to be competitive at the exhibition level, you're going to have to work at it. But don't worry—it's fun, and well worth it too.

As delightful as it is to eat fresh vegetables from the garden, it's equally fun to enter them at the county fair!

Selecting Specimens for Show

Obviously, you want to select the best specimens for exhibition.

Follow the rules as outlined in your fair rule book. If the rules say that all produce exhibits are to be presented on white paper plates, don't try to stand out from the crowd by using a paper plate with a colorful floral design; it's not going to help you. In fact, it might get you disqualified. If the rules say "three green peppers," make sure that you enter exactly three. Not two extra-large ones or four super-small ones; you want to enter three green peppers of uniform size. Stick to the rules and concentrate on entering the best-quality produce that you have.

Freedom from blemishes is an important characteristic of prize-winning produce, so be sure to fully examine each and every side of the vegetables that you're planning to enter. Don't overlook a large hole or an unsightly blemish.

Different varieties of corn range from 55 days to 90 days for maturation. If you plan to exhibit your corn at the fair, be sure to check the growing time and plant accordingly.

You want your exhibits to be fully ripe—meaning that they should be their proper mature color and size. Avoid entering green tomatoes (unless you're entering a specific category that calls for these), beans that are not fully grown, or carrots that are only an inch long.

If you're growing rare heirloom varieties in unusual colors or shapes, you may find that some judges are unfamiliar with those varieties. When observing the judging of open class exhibitions at county fairs, we have seen "unusual" specimens passed by in favor of more traditional ones. For instance, we know a girl who entered the Jimmy Nardello variety of sweet green pepper at her county fair. Now, Jimmy Nardellos are shaped like hot peppers; they are long and thin and angular—not at all like a traditional sweet bell pepper. She entered her exhibit in the sweet green

pepper category, just as she should have, but it was disqualified because they were "hot peppers." This was a mistake on the part of the judge and unfortunate for everyone involved, but it bears keeping in mind. Don't be surprised if a judge isn't familiar with every possible variety of each and every vegetable. Don't let it discourage you from entering rare varieties, either, but just be prepared.

Uniformity is important. Now, obviously, if you're entering one large zucchini squash, there isn't anything for it to be uniform *with*, but if you're entering any category in which more than one specimen is required, then try your hardest to select uniform examples.

For instance, if your class list calls for ten pods of peas, try to select ten pods that are exactly the same length,

The date of your county fair should always be in the back of your mind—you want to plant your vegetables at the proper time so that they will be mature for the fair. *Shutterstock*

It's All About You

It's a well-established fact for fair-entrants: Your vegetable exhibits need to have been grown by you. This means that they cannot have been grown by your grandma or your neighbors, and they cannot—under any circumstances—have been purchased at a grocery store or farmers' market. Your own hard work must have been the driving force behind the production of your vegetable exhibits. Don't ever try to pass off someone else's vegetables as your own.

Select only the very best produce for exhibition.

Good Things Come in Small(er) Packages

You may believe that the largest specimens are the best choices for exhibition, but this is not necessarily true. Unless you're entering a class specifically designed for large specimens ("Squash, Zucchini, Largest," for instance), then a display of average-size vegetables would be considered a better choice. Generally speaking, medium-size vegetables are considered more marketable than their larger counterparts. Large vegetables tend to lose flavor and are often considered to be past their prime, so keep this in mind when selecting specimens for exhibit.

width, depth, and color. Don't pick your three biggest pods to show them off and then fill in the other seven spaces with smaller pods. The three impressive pods are not going to compensate for the seven mismatched examples. You're much better off selecting ten pods that are all the same healthy size, even if they aren't as large as your impressive specimens.

Peas are relatively easy because they all mature to approximately the same shape. But what of peppers? As anyone who has grown peppers is aware, they don't all end up looking exactly the same, so you'll have to do your best to select the most uniform specimens that you have available in your garden, judging on color and size rather than shape.

Judges evaluate the exhibits on a wide variety of merits. Let's go over a few of them, which will hopefully help you in selecting the very best specimens for show. (Remember, these are general guidelines; refer to your own fair rulebook for specific judging criteria.)

This is a Jimmy Nardello heirloom pepper, and although it looks as though it might be a hot pepper, it's actually a sweet variety. If you decide to enter unusual heirloom varieties at the fair, you might want to ask the show secretary if you can make a notation on your entry form, explaining that it is an unusual type.

TIP

Uniformity is important. If your class list calls for ten pods of peas, try to select ten pods that are exactly the same length, width, depth, and color. Don't pick your three biggest pods to show them off and then fill in the other seven spaces with smaller pods.

Marketable Size: A tiny zucchini squash is not likely to sell at market—nor is it likely to place well at your fair. Exhibits should be comparable in size to something you would consider purchasing at the grocery store or farmers' market. This does not mean, however, that largest is always best (see "Good Things Come in Small(er) Packages" above).

Uniformity counts! Take a close look at these entries. Note the ones that received blue ribbons, red ribbons, or did not place. The blue ribbon–winning entries display excellent uniformity.

Characteristic Color. This is where you can get into trouble when exhibiting heirlooms. Your lovely Cherokee Purple heirloom tomatoes may be perfectly ripe and perfectly beautiful, but they'll only be competitive if the judge recognizes them for what they are. Perhaps your fair only offers classes for Red Tomatoes, Green Tomatoes, Golden Tomatoes, and Cherry Tomatoes. Where, then, do you enter Cherokee Purples? If you go ahead and enter them in the Red Tomato category, you could possibly be disqualified or discounted because your exhibit does not display characteristic color. It may be permissible to include a short note with your entry, explaining the situation. Check with your fair secretary ahead of time.

As you can see, two of these pumpkins received first-place blue ribbons, while the third pumpkin received only a second-place red ribbon. The differences in marketable size and stage of maturity are obvious.

Typical Shape. This category has similar caveats to characteristic color, since so many rare heirlooms are unusually shaped. However, aside from this, shape is important. Your entry may place lower if your carrots are abnormally crooked or your peppers are oddly shaped.

Stage of Development or Maturity. If your exhibits are tiny and not quite mature, you may find your score and placing lowered.

Cleanliness. A dirty vegetable is terribly unappetizing at the table and not appealing to a judge, either. You are exhibiting, after all, so take the time to gently clean or lightly wash your produce before taking it to the fair. Large clumps of dirt or mud splatterings just don't belong on your prize-winning exhibits.

Proper Trimming. Along with cleanliness, a neat and tidy appearance is also appreciated by judges. Trim off anything unsightly or unnecessary.

Freshness. Harvest your vegetables as close as possible to show day. Freshness is one of the criteria upon which your vegetables are judged—so don't take shriveled-up veggies and expect them to win.

Mechanical Injury. Whacks from an unwieldy hoe or shovel can leave blemishes on your vegetables. Points can be deducted for the presence of mechanical injury; this includes broken stems too.

Pests. Peppers with holes, zucchini with tiny bites from a squirrel's mouth—these blemishes from pests can also count for deductions. Choose pest-free specimens for show.

Uniformity. As we discussed previously, uniformity of appearance is very important, and this includes uniformity of *type or variety*. This is important. You'll earn more points if you enter a plate of four Brandywine tomatoes rather than two Brandywines, one Early Girl, and one Beefsteak. Uniformity of size and maturity is also important—as is uniformity of shape and color.

It's important to bring only the freshest of vegetables for exhibition—this is even more vital when exhibiting herbs.

So many pumpkins—can you choose the best one? The judge at your county fair will have to select the best specimens from dozens of entries.

This tomato has reached an impressive size, but its color indicates that it is far from mature.

Though still not entirely mature, this is a better stage for exhibition at the fair.

Displays are a great way to share the joys of gardening with people at the fair. This attractive display is eye-catching and impressive.

Bring Extra and Other Tips

Let's say that the rule book for your county fair requires five specimens for a sweet pepper exhibit. So you select five wonderful peppers for your entry and take them along to the fair. Unbeknownst to you, Fido isn't just sitting quietly in the back seat of the car as you travel to the fair; Fido has been helping himself to a bit of a snack. You arrive at the fair and discover that you only have three peppers left and Fido has pepper breath. Now what?

This is where we can give you a very helpful piece of advice: Always bring extra. If the rule book calls for five peppers, bring a couple of extra. If you're planning to exhibit an entry of three tomatoes, bring five. This way, if anything unexpected happens en route to the fair, your project isn't completely ruined. Unfortunately, the excuse "the dog ate my peppers" works just about as well at the fair as it does at school. If all goes well, you can just take the extras home with you and eat them instead.

More tidbits: Avoid placing your produce exhibits in sealed plastic bags as you transport them to the fair; they need airflow. Sometimes a fair will provide presentation materials for your produce, while other fairs require you to provide your own. In either case, refer to your rule book for the pertinent information that you'll need to prepare your exhibits.

Doing Your Best

Ronny and Blake are both working on their garden projects with the ambition of entering produce in the county fair at the end of the summer. But their gardening styles are very different. Ronny spends a couple of hours each day tending to his plants; weeding, watering, and working, while Blake works in his garden once or twice a week if he remembers. He ignores most of the weeds and relies on the rain to water his plants.

At harvest time, Ronny has a very nice crop of tomatoes, and on the morning of entry day he selects the four nicest specimens to take to the fair. He chooses uniform sizes and gently cleans them with a damp cloth before taking them to the fair, where he presents them on a white paper plate (as required in his fair rule book).

On the other hand, three or four days before entry day, Blake rummages through his tomato plants and finally finds four scrawny tomatoes. Although they are still green, Blake picks them anyway. His tomatoes have no chance of winning, due to their immaturity and small size.

The end of the story? Ronny's tomatoes place second in a very large class and Blake's are disqualified for their poor condition.

It isn't always precisely this way, but generally speaking, your prizes will be relative to the amount of time and effort that you expend for your gardening projects. Take the time to do a good job so that you can enter produce that you can be proud of.

Remember!

You want to harvest the majority of your vegetables as close to fair day as possible, but there is one exception: onions. Because onions need time to dry, it's not advisable to harvest them immediately prior to your date of exhibition. Instead, harvest your onions at least two weeks ahead of time. This will allow your onions the opportunity to dry well.

Another tip: Don't peel all of the layers of skin from your onions before the show. It's okay to remove the outer peeling if it's particularly dirty, but other than this, leave the skins on.

A lot of work goes into preparing vegetable exhibits—they're the end result of months of care and nurturing. It's quite an accomplishment!

Preparing a Garden Box

A garden box (also known as a market basket, market box, or garden basket) is essentially a large presentation of vegetables from your garden. Typically, the fair rule book will outline a wide variety of choices from which you will select approximately six to comprise your box.

Possibilities Might Include:

- 2 heads of broccoli
- 2 heads of cabbage
- 2 heads of cauliflower
- 6 carrots
- 6 onions
- 12 green beans
- 2 cucumbers
- 4 tomatoes
- 4 peppers
- 2 squash

The beauty of this is that you can select only the six vegetables that are your best examples, so if your cucumber crop was poor, you could simply avoid that one and select something else from the list. A garden box can make an impressive presentation for your county fair—and a fun one, too.

Additionally, the rules may also change in relation to your level of gardening expertise. A novice gardener could enter a class that required only four types of vegetables in a garden box, while a second-year exhibitor might enter a class that includes six types of vegetables.

Your county fair might also require a combination of large and medium vegetables: perhaps one pumpkin, one watermelon, and one cabbage, along with five peppers, five tomatoes, and five carrots. The rules vary widely, so check your fair book for the official criteria for entries.

What If I Don't Win?

After a summer of watering, weeding, hoeing, thinning, and mulching, the fair has arrived. You've selected your best specimens, gently washed and prepared them, and now the hour of judging has arrived. And you receive fourth place.

Ouch.

Losing a class is never fun, never easy, and always a little discouraging. You might ask yourself, "What did I do wrong?"

Perhaps nothing. In a large class of entries, perhaps the other higher-placed entries were of a more marketable size, perhaps they were more uniform in color and shape, or perhaps they were cleaner or fresher. You may have done your best, but it just wasn't quite enough to bring home the top prize this time around.

The amount of effort that you put into your gardening project typically correlates to the quality of the produce that you'll harvest.

Whatever you do, don't let it discourage you from entering again. A prize at the fair is merely the icing on the cake, the culmination, shall we say, of your summer of hard work. But the lessons learned, the knowledge gained, the intrinsic reward of setting a goal and accomplishing it—these are values that are worth more than any ribbon. Cherish them! (And then go and have a delicious salad of homegrown vegetables!)

It's sometimes difficult to select the best specimens to enter at the fair. There are many aspects to consider.

Chapter 8

Preserving Your Harvest

One thing about gardens—they don't always cooperate with what's easiest for you. While it would be nice to have a steady stream of ripened produce coming into the kitchen, it's rarely as convenient as that. Instead, you'll have seventeen zucchini squashes ready at the same time, or five pints of green beans, or forty-nine tomatoes. As delicious as they are to eat fresh, it's not always possible to consume forty-nine tomatoes before they spoil. For this reason, we have preservation processes with which to save produce for future eating.

Saving for Later

The processes of drying, freezing, and canning are far too complicated to fully explain within the confines of this text, but here is a brief explanation of each:

- Drying is popular for fruits such as apples and pears but also very popular with beans. You can also dry peppers, okra, summer squash, and many other vegetables.

- Freezing is our personal favorite. It's ridiculously easy to freeze berries, corn, apples, and zucchini. Some vegetables such as green beans and peas require blanching (lightly cooking at a rapid boil) prior to freezing, but this, too, is an easy step and well worth the effort for the reward that you gain: perfectly ripe, "picked at the peak of perfection" vegetables that cook up beautifully for delightful winter eating.

- Canning is a long-favored procedure for preserving foods, but it requires quite a bit of equipment and know-how in order to do it correctly. Seek the advice of a knowledgeable friend or relative to teach you the process.

Harvest time—a glorious time of year! But what will you do with all of your garden produce? *iStockphoto.com/Mark Jensen*

Preserving your harvest can be accomplished by drying, freezing, or canning. These onions are drying in the late summer sun, and can then be stored in a cool, dark place for several months.

Seed Saving

If you've raised heirloom (open pollinated, not hybrid) vegetables, then you may want to consider saving some of their seed for your next garden. It sounds simple, doesn't it? Saving seeds—how involved could it be, anyway? It's true that seed saving isn't particularly difficult or time-consuming, but it does require a certain amount of know-how in order to achieve success. If you don't know the basics, you're sure to run into some roadblocks.

Things to consider:

It's important to understand the characteristics of the particular vegetable from which you wish to save seeds. You must understand the type of pollination it requires (is it self-pollinated, wind pollinated, or insect pollinated?), as well as whether or not the plants need to be isolated from other varieties to avoid cross-pollination. You'll also need to know if the vegetable produces seed annually or biennially. You could wait all season for a particular vegetable to produce seed, but if it's a biennial, it won't produce until the second season.

The procedures for saving seeds vary depending on the type of vegetable. The process for drying and saving

TIP

We love saving bean seeds; they're so plump and impressive it really feels like you're saving something important.

Many vegetables, including these green beans, should be blanched prior to freezing.

These beans have been blanched and then placed in heavy-duty freezer bags, ready to be frozen for future use.

tomato seeds is vastly different from the process of saving seeds from a green bean. (As an aside, we love saving bean seeds; they're so plump and impressive it really feels like you're saving something important.)

Research the necessary information about your vegetable varieties before attempting to save seed.

Marketing Your Excess Produce

Perhaps you have an abundance of extra produce—more than you can easily consume, save, or disperse among your friends. Perhaps you'd like to earn a bit of extra money to put toward your garden project next

Saving heirloom seeds is an excellent end-of-summer project.

Sunflower seeds are easy to save and a lot of fun to harvest. Have a sunflower-seed party and collect them all!

year. If any of these are true, then you may want to consider marketing your vegetables for sale.

The most familiar way of marketing homegrown vegetables is to set up at a farmers' market. Many communities have a weekly farmers' market, so all you need to do is contact the coordinator for details on how to become involved. There is typically a small fee involved with setting up at the market for a day, but this small investment can be easily recouped by your sales at the market.

Setting Up Your Booth

Your booth can be as simple or as elaborate as you choose. A small tent can be very nice, as it offers the protection of shade, which is more comfortable for you and your customers—and better for your produce too. If a tent isn't an option, make sure that you wear a large hat and plenty of sunscreen. In either case, you'll need a portable table (or two) on which to display your vegetables. A pretty tablecloth is always a plus; you want your stand to be attractive and eye-catching, and you want people to come and take a look at your offerings. You might bring along some baskets in which to display your vegetables. Always remember to bring cash with which to make change for your customers. It's not convenient for your customers if you don't have ample change. And don't forget to bring a chair and a good book!

To sell your farm produce, your first stop will likely be your local farmers' market.

Baskets and boxes will help keep your vegetables organized at the farmers' market.

Don't forget your fruits! Baskets of apples, pints of berries, clusters of grapes—there's no end to the marketing possibilities.

Signs

As you plan for your market stand, pay special attention to your signs. Your signs are one of the most important parts of your market stand. Ideally, your signs will be large enough to be easily legible, as well as clearly explaining the type of produce that you're offering.

Top tips for great signs:

- **Less is more:** "HEIRLOOM TOMATOES, $1 EACH" in large letters is more concise and effective than "YOU'VE COME TO THE RIGHT PLACE! BUNCHES OF HEIRLOOM TOMATOES AND THEY TASTE GREAT TOO AND YOU SHOULD BUY SOME FOR YOUR GRANDMOTHER AND YOUR AUNT SUE BECAUSE THEY ARE ONLY $1 EACH" in small letters.

- **Spelling counts:** Watch your spelling and punctuation. You're aiming to project an appearance of professionalism, and if your sign says "FRESH TAMATOS and BEENS," people are less likely to take you seriously.

- **Contrasting colors:** If you are using yellow poster board for your sign, then you wouldn't want to use orange lettering—it would be too difficult to read, especially at a distance. In the same manner, if your poster board is white, then you'll want to use a lettering that is dark and easy to read from far away. If people can't read your sign easily, they won't be as likely to come and view your produce.

Oops—"Punkins" isn't the correct spelling. Always make sure that everything is spelled properly.

Much better! Attention to detail is important, even when making farmers' market signs.

Pricing

It can be difficult to know exactly how to price your vegetables for sale. On one hand, who can put a price on the hours of hard work and effort that you've put into your garden? On the other hand, who's going to pay $75 for a single cucumber?

To get an idea of the prices of produce in your local area, visit your farmers' market before you set up your own stand. Look around at all of the stands, and compare the prices of vegetables. You'll see a lot of variation. Some of the prices will probably be lower than you would like to charge; some of the others might be more than you had considered asking. Consider all of this information and then settle on prices that seem fair and satisfactory to you. After your first week at the market, you'll have a better idea of whether you're asking too much or too little. If you sold out all of your produce in the first hour, then your prices might be too low. On the other hand, if you haven't sold much at all, your prices might be too high (or else you have really crummy produce, but you'll have to figure that one out for yourself).

Preparing Your Produce

Presentation is important. No one wants to purchase food that is unappealing to look at. For this reason, make sure that all of your produce is super-fresh and gently cleaned. Don't pull up your carrots from the garden and toss them in a basket to sell, covered with scraggly roots and dirt. Take a few moments to brush or wipe each one clean, then trim the extra roots. These small steps will help make your vegetables more appealing to customers and will likely result in extra sales for you. Small details make a difference.

Pricing your vegetables can be difficult. Take some time to compare prices at other farmers' market vendors. Are their vegetables priced much higher or lower than yours?

You can price your vegetables by weight, as shown here, or simply by number—tomatoes, two for $1.00, for instance.

Farm Stands

Maybe you don't have a local farmers' market—or maybe you do, but getting to it once a week just isn't feasible during the busy summer months. Then again, maybe you don't need a farmers' market: You might be able to set up a roadside farm stand on your own property.

There are a couple of caveats. First of all, people have to be able to find you. If your farm is in a remote location, the daily traffic going past your home is probably negligible, and the number of potential customers is likely even smaller. You don't want your harvest to get shriveled and inedible waiting for customers who never arrive. However, if you live in a populated area with good visibility, then a farm stand may be just the ticket to selling some of your excess produce.

Another consideration: the legalities. Some county and town zoning ordinances prohibit even the part-time sale of farm products from a roadside stand on your property. Consult your town code of ordinances to make sure that your farm stand is not infringing on any regulations.

Once you've cleared those two hurdles, it's time to consider the logistics of your farm stand. Signage is just as important as it is with a farmers' market, so be sure that your signs are effective and clear, with good color contrast and visibility. Make a few decisions about the frequency with which you will operate your stand. Will it be open every Saturday? Every Monday? Every morning? Will you personally man the booth, or will you leave the produce with a cash box on the honor system? These are questions that you and your family will have to answer before beginning your endeavor.

You may be able to ask higher prices for rare or unusual varieties, such as these red Dragon heirloom carrots.

The picture of cleanliness! These tomatoes are just asking to be purchased. They're shiny and clean and simply appetizing.

A farm stand can be a great way to market your produce without leaving home.

Chapter 9

Enjoying Your Harvest

Gardening and cooking go hand in hand. There are many delightful treats that you can prepare with the produce from your vegetable garden. Even if cooking isn't something that typically piques your interest, you'll want to experiment as the harvest rolls in. We've gathered a few recipes that anyone can enjoy preparing. These four recipes are simple and delicious, and they utilize the vegetables and fruits that you've harvested. You'll enjoy making these classic dishes for years to come.

A beautiful sight—a kitchen counter filled with fresh garden vegetables! *Shutterstock*

Heirloom Tomato Salad

SERVES 4

6 medium heirloom tomatoes
salad dressing or extra-virgin olive oil, to taste
3 heirloom sweet peppers (*optional*)
1 heirloom cucumber (*optional*)
1 onion (*optional*)

The fun of this salad is that it's never the same twice. As the season progresses, the varieties that compose these salads evolve, but they're always colorful, always interesting, and always delicious.

In the early summer, we rely on the trustworthy, early-producing Stupice variety, intermixed with the first Mexico Midgets and Beam's Yellow Pears. As the weeks pass, we begin adding more color, via the dusky purple Cherokee Purples, the rosy German Pinks, and the zesty Green Zebras.

To make your own salad, begin with freshly picked heirloom tomatoes. Medium and large tomatoes should be chopped into small pieces; cherry tomatoes can be tossed in without cutting. Chill before serving, and add the salad dressing of your choice as desired. Alternately, you can toss the tomatoes with a touch of extra-virgin olive oil. It's simple, easy, and ever-so-good.

If you also have heirloom sweet peppers or cucumbers ready at the same time, by all means, add them in as well. A bit of onion is another excellent addition. These extra flavors and textures make your heirloom salads even better—but if all you have ready at the moment are tomatoes, never fear; they can stand on their own, very well in fact.

We know what you're thinking: "But I only planted hybrid tomatoes! Can I still make the salad?" Of course! Absolutely. We just happen to like the varying colors and flavors of heirlooms.

Apple Blackberry Crisp

SERVES 12

8 large baking apples
2 cups fresh blackberries
½ cup white granulated sugar
½ cup brown sugar
1½ cups rolled oats
½ cup butter
vanilla ice cream (optional)

This is a dessert beyond compare. The very name conjures up images of glorious late-summer afternoons and the sweet scent of baked apples.

It's also as easy as can be to make, especially for people like us who think that any recipe with more than five ingredients is simply too hard to bother with. This recipe is simple and delicious—we guarantee it.

Preheat the oven to 350 degrees Fahrenheit. Start with eight large baking apples, washed, peeled, and sliced. McIntosh or Granny Smith can be good choices. For this dish, we try to avoid "eating" varieties such as Golden Delicious; they get a bit soft when baked. Toss the slices into a greased 9 × 12-inch baking dish. Next, wash the blackberries, and add them to the dish with the apples.

Sprinkle the white sugar directly over the fruit. In a separate bowl, stir together the brown sugar and the rolled oats (don't use the instant kind). Then take the butter (either melted or cut into tiny pieces) and add it into the oat mixture. Mix this thoroughly, and then pour the oat mixture over the top of your apples and blackberries in the baking dish. Make sure that the apples and blackberries are thoroughly covered with the oat mixture, and then pop the entire dish in the oven.

Baking time will vary, depending on the type of apples that you're using (some varieties cook up much faster than others). Figure on at least 35 minutes; you may need up to 45 if your apples are still firm after 35 minutes. Watch for the bubbling of the juices along the edge of the dish; this is a good indication that the crisp is nearly finished.

Serve warm or cold, with or without ice cream. Delightful!

Roasted Vegetables

SERVES 8

8 large potatoes and/or sweet potatoes
2 large or 6 small onions
4 to 6 carrots
2 to 3 tbsp olive oil
salt and pepper to taste
fresh herbs (*optional*)

This is another of our favorites because it's so ridiculously simple to make and so deliciously wonderful to eat. Figure on making this at the end of the summer, once you've harvested your potatoes and/or your sweet potatoes and your onions are dry. (This recipe is fun because you can modify it with whatever vegetables you happen to have handy and in ample amounts, such as bell peppers or summer squash.) Experiment to discover your favorite combinations!

Preheat the oven to 400 degrees Fahrenheit. Prepare a large baking dish—the bigger the better. We like to line the baking dish with aluminum foil, as this helps make cleanup easier.

Wash and peel your potatoes or sweet potatoes, and chop into 2-inch pieces. Peel and wash your onions, then slice them into large pieces. Do the same for the handful of carrots. Place all of the potatoes, onions, and carrots in the baking dish. Next, take 2 to 3 tablespoons of olive oil and drizzle it evenly over the top of the vegetables. Salt and pepper as desired, or you can add in any complementary herbs, such as rosemary or oregano, that you might have ready to use. Pop the dish in the oven and cook for 60 to 90 minutes, stirring occasionally to redistribute the vegetables. Serve piping hot and enjoy—roasted vegetables are simply divine!

Zucchini Bread

SERVES 8

2 cups shredded or chopped zucchini

1½ cups flour

½ cup white sugar

½ cup brown sugar

1 tsp baking soda

1 tsp salt

¼ cup butter

½ cup milk

1 egg

1 to 2 overripe bananas (optional)

We've been perfecting this recipe for years. It seems like every year we make another small adjustment to the recipe in order to make it as perfect as possible. We think we're pretty close.

This is a great recipe for anyone with an overabundance of zucchini squash (yes, we see you raising your hand). It's a simply delicious way to use up zucchini. And for those of you who don't care for the taste of zucchini, you almost don't know it's in here.

Preheat the oven to 350 degrees Fahrenheit. Start off by preparing your zucchini—you'll need shredded or finely chopped zucchini. Set that aside. In a mixing bowl, blend the flour, white sugar, brown sugar, baking soda, and salt. Then add the butter, milk, and egg. Mix thoroughly, and then add in the zucchini. Continue mixing. Grease and flour a loaf pan and place your bread mixture directly into the pan. For a fun added twist, add in a mashed overripe banana or two into the bread mixture before you pop it in the oven—the zucchini and banana are very tasty together.

Bake in the oven for about 55 minutes.

Make Your Own Pizza Garden

If you're like us, you love pizza. And what's better than a made-from-scratch pizza, with ingredients that you grew in your garden? For this project, you'll want to plant a nice selection of tomato and pepper plants—look for heirloom varieties for the best rainbow of color and range of flavors—and then plant plenty of onions. A couple of basil and oregano plants are also a good idea; rosemary can also be a nice choice. If you want to get truly creative, prepare a circle-shaped garden bed with dividers (to look like pizza slices). Plant one type of vegetable or herb in each division. Later in the summer, you can host a pizza party and make pizzas with ingredients that you literally grew yourself. What fun!

Enjoy the vegetables of your labor.

Appendix 1

Glossary

annual: A plant that lives for only one season. Most vegetable plants are annuals.

biennial: A plant, such as parsley, that survives for two growing seasons.

bolting: The process of a plant going to seed. Lettuce and spinach are prone to bolting if you don't harvest them in time.

clay soil: A type of soil that is very heavy and retains a great deal of water.

cold frame: Essentially a miniature greenhouse, designed to protect sensitive plants in the early spring or late fall.

community garden: A large public garden space that is shared by members of a community; work and produce are shared.

companion planting: The process of planting two different vegetables near each other for mutual benefit, such as pole beans next to corn, which allows the beans to climb the corn stalks.

compost: A type of organic soil builder and fertilizer that comprises a mixture of natural substances, such as dried leaves, kitchen scraps, and farm animal manure.

crop rotation: The process of alternating the locations of your garden vegetables from year to year. This is beneficial to prevent plant diseases from recurring.

determinate: A tomato variety that grows to a limited plant size and sets its fruit more or less all at once.

double-cropping: The process of planting a late-season crop (such as zucchini) in the same location where an early-season crop (such as snow peas) has already been harvested, thus obtaining "double" the crops from that space in a single year.

flats: The sets of tiny plastic "cells" in which seeds are often started indoors.

frost-free date: The average last date of frost for a gardening zone.

full sun: A minimum of eight to ten hours of sunlight per day.

garden box: A popular county fair exhibit that consists of a large presentation of many different vegetables.

germination time: The time from planting a seed until it sprouts.

growing season: The length of time between the last frost of spring and the first frost of autumn.

hardening off: The process of gradually acclimating seedlings to the outdoors before planting.

hardiness zone: The United States Department of Agriculture's designation for the various climates; a useful way to select plants that are suitably hardy for your region.

heirloom: A variety of vegetable, usually open pollinated, that has been in cultivation for many generations. Heirlooms are prized for their distinctive flavors, colors, and shapes.

hill: A raised area or mound approximately 12 to 24 inches in diameter and 4 to 8 inches high, for planting certain vegetables, particularly squash or cucumbers.

hybrid: A plant that is the product of two genetically different plants. Hybrids are bred for traits such as disease resistance or fast maturation.

indeterminate: A tomato variety that grows taller and expands throughout the growing season and bears fruit for many weeks.

inorganic fertilizer: A type of fertilizer that is derived from synthetic chemical sources.

integrated pest management (IPM): The process of eliminating garden pests with minimal use of chemicals.

intercropping: The practice of planting more than one crop in a particular area, such as radishes and carrots in a single row.

loam soil: The ideal garden soil: a nice, loose, fluffy soil without too much sand or clay.

mulching: The process of adding mulch (grass clippings, wood shavings, hay, or straw) to gently cover the ground around plants. Mulching helps keep the soil moist and weeds at bay.

open pollinated: Nonhybrid; a plant that has the ability to reproduce itself without the assistance of humans.

organic fertilizer: A type of fertilizer that is derived from natural sources, such as plants or animal manure.

partial sun: Less than eight hours of sun each day.

peat pot: A small pot that is used for transplanting seedlings directly into the garden without disturbing the roots.

perennial: A plant that survives for longer than two growing seasons. Asparagus and rhubarb are perennials, as are chives and most fruits.

pH: A measurement of a soil's acidity (4.5–6.8) or alkalinity (7.5–8.0). Neutral soil has a pH of 7.0.

raised bed: An elevated garden plot; typically made of wood and about 4 × 8 feet.

root crop: Vegetables we grow for their edible roots. Carrots, radishes, beets, potatoes, and parsnips are all examples of root crops.

sandy soil: A type of loose soil that is composed of mainly sand; sandy soil does not hold water well.

side dressing: Also known as top dressing; the act of adding fertilizer to the top of the soil after planting.

succession planting: The process of planting the same vegetable more than once throughout the growing season in order to be able to continually harvest a particular vegetable for many weeks.

thinning: The process of removing excess seedlings from a row in order to make room for the remaining seedlings to fully mature. Thinning is essential for carrots and beets.

trellis: A type of lattice that is suitable for plants to climb; trellises can be made of wood, plastic, metal, or bamboo stakes.

Appendix 2

Hardiness Zones

Perhaps you've noticed them in seed catalogs—color-coded maps that define the climate zone of each location in North America. The United States Department of Agriculture (USDA) issues a hardiness zone map that recognizes eleven different zones (ten of which are divided into subzones). Zone maps from other sources may vary slightly in appearance, but the general idea is the same. Lower zone numbers like 2, 3, and 4 represent cold, northern areas with fairly short growing seasons and low average minimum temperatures. Higher zone numbers such as 8, 9, or 10 are warm, southern locations with long growing seasons. Other environmental features such as mountains, annual weather patterns, and large bodies of water also affect a location's zone number. Once you have found out your zone, you'll be able to select plants and seeds that are suitably hardy to survive winters in your climate. For instance, if you live in Zone 4, you would only want to purchase plants and seeds that are hardy to Zones 1 to 4; if a particular plant is only hardy to Zone 5, you may not want to risk planting it in your garden.

There are exceptions, of course. Let's say that Bert is starting his garden. When he checks the hardiness zone map, he discovers that his area is in Zone 4—but just barely. Bert's local area is in a small pocket of Zone 4 within a region that is otherwise almost entirely Zone 3. So though he might succeed with plants that are hardy in Zone 4, he should play it safe and opt mostly for plants that are perennial in Zone 3 instead.

Most vegetables (including tomatoes) are annuals, which means you don't have to worry about whether or not they'll survive in your zone—they die at the end of the growing season. But if you are planting perennial fruits or herbs, be careful to choose varieties that will survive in your hardiness zone.

USDA Hardiness Zones
and Average Annual Minimum Temperature Range

ZONE	FAHRENHEIT	CELSIUS	EXAMPLE CITIES
1A/B	Below -50°F	Below -45.6°C	Fairbanks, Alaska; Resolute, Northwest Territories (Canada)
2A	-50 to -45°F	-42.8 to -45.5°C	Prudhoe Bay, Alaska; Flin Flon, Manitoba (Canada)
2B	-45 to -40°F	-40.0 to -42.7°C	Unalakleet, Alaska; Pinecreek, Minnesota
3A	-40 to -35°F	-37.3 to -39.9°C	International Falls, Minnesota; St. Michael, Alaska
3B	-35 to -30°F	-34.5 to -37.2°C	Tomahawk, Wisconsin; Sidney, Montana
4A	-30 to -25°F	-31.7 to -34.4°C	Minneapolis/St.Paul, Minnesota; Lewistown, Montana
4B	-25 to -20°F	-28.9 to -31.6°C	Northwood, Iowa; Nebraska
5A	-20 to -15°F	-26.2 to -28.8°C	Des Moines, Iowa; Illinois
5B	-15 to -10°F	-23.4 to -26.1°C	Columbia, Missouri; Mansfield, Pennsylvania
6A	-10 to -5°F	-20.6 to -23.3°C	St. Louis, Missouri; Lebanon, Pennsylvania
6B	-5 to 0°F	-17.8 to -20.5°C	McMinnville, Tennessee; Branson, Missouri
7A	0 to 5°F	-15.0 to -17.7°C	Oklahoma City, Oklahoma; South Boston, Virginia
7B	5 to 10°F	-12.3 to -14.9°C	Little Rock, Arkansas; Griffin, Georgia
8A	10 to 15°F	-9.5 to -12.2°C	Tifton, Georgia; Dallas, Texas
8B	15 to 20°F	-6.7 to -9.4°C	Austin, Texas; Gainesville, Florida
9A	20 to 25°F	-3.9 to -6.6°C	Houston, Texas; St. Augustine, Florida
9B	25 to 30°F	-1.2 to -3.8°C	Brownsville, Texas; Fort Pierce, Florida
10A	30 to 35°F	1.6 to -1.1°C	Naples, Florida; Victorville, California
10B	35 to 40°F	4.4 to 1.7°C	Miami, Florida; Coral Gables, Florida
11A/B	above 40°F	above 4.5°C	Honolulu, Hawaii; Mazatlan, Mexico

Courtesy U.S. National Arboretum, Agricultural Research Service, U.S. Department of Agriculture, Washington, DC 20002

Plant Hardiness Zone Map

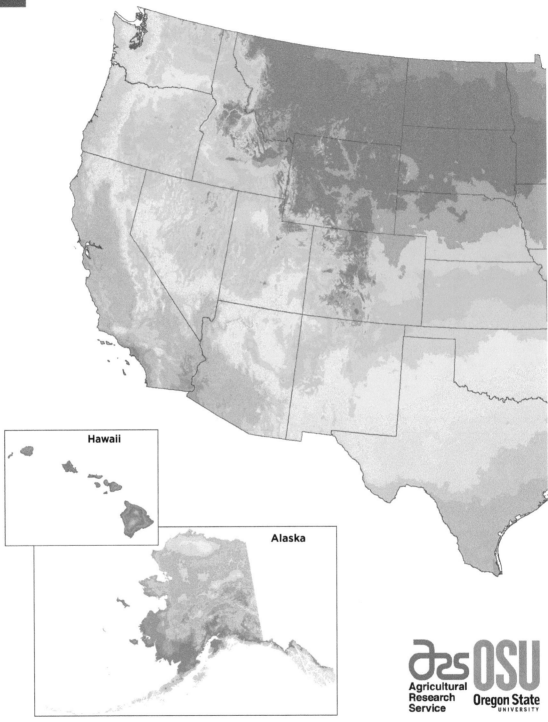

Hawaii

Alaska

Agricultural Research Service

Oregon State UNIVERSITY

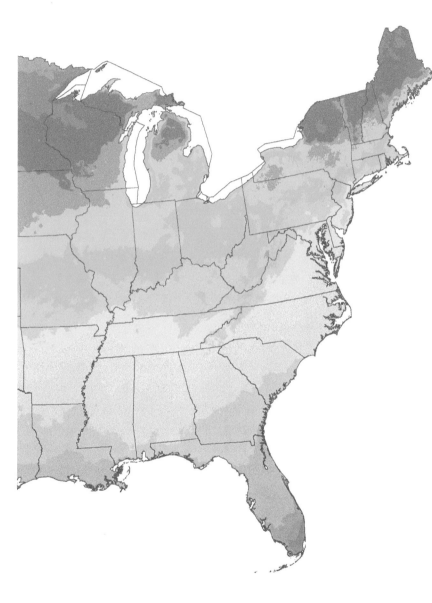

Average Annual Extreme Minimum Teperatur 1976-2005

Temp (F)	Zone	Temp (C)
-60 to -55	1a	-51.1 to -48.3
-55 to -50	1b	-48.3 to -45.6
-50 to -45	2a	-45.6 to -42.8
-45 to -40	2b	-42.8 to -40
-40 to -35	3a	-40 to -37.2
-35 to -30	3b	-37.2 to -34.4
-30 to -25	4a	-34.4 to -31.7
-25 to -20	4b	-31.7 to -28.9
-20 to -15	5a	-28.9 to -26.1
-15 to -10	5b	-26.1 to -23.3
-10 to -5	6a	-23.3 to -20.6
-5 to 0	6b	-20.6 to -17.8
0 to 5	7a	-17.8 to -15
5 to 10	7b	-15 to -12.2
10 to 15	8a	-12.2 to -9.4
15 to 20	8b	-9.4 to -6.7
20 to 25	9a	-6.7 to -3.9
25 to 30	9b	-3.9 to -1.1
30 to 35	10a	-1.1 to 1.7
35 to 40	10b	1.7 to 4.4
40 to 45	11a	4.4 to 7.2
45 to 50	11b	7.2 to 10
50 to 55	12a	10 to 12.8
55 to 60	12b	12.8 to 15.6
60 to 65	13a	15.6 to 18.3
65 to 70	13b	18.3 to 21.1

Puerto Rico

Mapping by the
PRISM Climate Group,
Oregon State University,
http://prism.oregonstate.
edu, 2012

Appendix 3

Resources

4-H
www.4-h.org

Kids Gardening
www.kidsgardening.org

**National FFA Organization
(Future Farmers of America)**
www.ffa.org

National Gardening Association
www.garden.org (If you're on Facebook, you can "like" the National Gardening Association; they post daily tips and information that can be very helpful as you work on your garden project.)

Square Foot Gardening
www.squarefootgardening.com

USDA Plant Hardiness Zone Map
https://planthardiness.ars.usda.gov

Heirloom Seed Suppliers

Baker Creek Heirloom Seeds
www.rareseeds.com

Italian Seed and Tool Company
www.italianseedandtool.com

Renee's Garden
www.reneesgarden.com

Seed Savers Exchange
www.seedsavers.org

Seed Companies

Burpee
www.burpee.com

Gurney's
www.gurneys.com

Johnny's Selected Seeds
www.johnnyseeds.com

Jung's
www.jungseed.com

Park Seed
www.parkseed.com

Garden Supply Companies

Gardener's Supply Company
www.gardeners.com

Gardens Alive!
www.gardensalive.com

Lee Valley Tools
www.leevalley.com

Plow & Hearth
www.plowhearth.com

Index

About the Authors and Photographer

Daniel Johnson is a full-time professional writer and photographer whose images appear in books, magazines, calendars, and greeting cards. He photographs all aspects of farm life from gardening to livestock to farm kids and particularly enjoys photographing horses and dogs. As a 4-H alumnus, he enjoys helping young people with their projects. Dan lives on Fox Hill Farm in far northern Wisconsin where the vigorous winters and beautiful summers offer fantastic photo opportunities. Dan's work can be viewed at www.foxhillphoto.com or on the Fox Hill Farm blog at www.foxhillphoto.blogspot.com.

Samantha Johnson is the author of several books on horses and rabbits, and her articles have appeared in a number of national magazines. Samantha was a 4-H member for many years and has fond memories of county fair exhibits and other 4-H activities. She is a certified horse show judge and raises purebred Welsh mountain ponies in addition to her Dutch, Holland Lop, and Netherland Dwarf rabbits. She resides in northern Wisconsin where she enjoys vegetable gardening.